Contents

VGM Careers for You Series

CAREERS

F O R

FOREIGN LANGUAGE AFICIONADOS
& Other Multilingual Types

H. Ned Seelye
J. Laurence Day

Foreword by
C. Edward Scebold
Executive Director
American Council of Teachers of Foreign Languages

VGM Career Horizons
a division of *NTC Publishing Group*
Lincolnwood, Illinois USA

Library of Congress Cataloging-in-Publication Data
Seelye, H. Ned.
  Careers for foreign language aficionados & other multilingual
types/H. Ned Seelye, J. Laurence Day.
      p.   cm.—(VGM careers for you series)
      ISBN 0-8442-8130-1.—ISBN 0-8442-8129-8 (pbk.): $8.95
      1. Language and languages—Vocational guidance—United States.
I. Day, J. Laurence.   II. Title.   III. Series.
P60.2.U6S4   1991
402'.3'73—dc20   91-24617
                                                                          CIP

1994 Printing

Published by. VGM Career Horizons, a division of NTC Publishing Group.
© 1992 by NTC Publishing Group, 4255 West Touhy Avenue,
Lincolnwood (Chicago), Illinois 60646-1975 U.S.A.
Manufactured in the United States of America.

    4 5 6 7 8 9 0 VP 9 8 7 6 5 4 3

About the Authors

H. Ned Seelye quit high school at the end of his junior year and hitchhiked to Mexico to seek his fortune. In two weeks his future became clear: it was zilch. He didn't know Spanish, had no work permit, had no marketable skill (couldn't even type), and didn't know anybody in Mexico. It was time for Plan B. Seelye entered college on the basis of entrance exams (what other basis was there?), became fluent in Spanish, and acquired some marketable skills. Seelye specializes in inter-cultural communication and educational research (mostly in Third World settings) and has lived almost twenty years abroad. His international career includes projects in 30 countries of Europe, Africa, Asia, and Latin America. He has held many positions of responsibility, including Illinois State Foreign Language Supervisor, Illinois State Director of Bilingual Education, CEO of International Resource Development, Inc. (a social science research firm in LaGrange, Illinois), Associate Professor of Sociology and Anthropology, and Executive Director of the Spanish Education Development Center (Washington, D.C.). Seelye is listed in *Who's Who in International Education* and has lectured in over a dozen educational centers abroad.

J. Laurence Day joined the faculty of the Department of Communication Arts, University of West Florida, in 1988 after

22 years as professor at the William Allen White School of Journalism, University of Kansas. He earned B.A. and M.A. degrees at Brigham Young University, and a Ph.D. at the University of Minnesota. Day has been a UPI correspondent in Latin America, and a reporter and copy editor for U.S. metropolitan newspapers. His career research interests include professionalization of Latin American journalists, and international news flow, about which he has published extensively. He has won two senior Fulbright lectureships, taught at some 15 universities in Latin America, and has conducted workshops for journalists throughout Latin America and the Caribbean. In 1990 he was on the team that produced "Giving Up the Canal," a television documentary on Panama. In 1991 he traveled with the team to Havana to work on a Cuban documentary. His most recent research efforts produced, in collaboration with H. Ned Seelye, 18 anti-drug abuse comic books.

Acknowledgments

The authors would like to acknowledge the help given to them by Kathy Siebel, able editor for NTC Publishing Group, and by Tony Simmons, Matt Nickerson, and Geri Critchley.

Foreword

Today it was the Indian couple ahead of me on a flight to Denver speaking Hindi. Yesterday it was the television broadcast from Moscow, and the day before it was Hasidic Jews in Brooklyn. In each instance I got someone else's synopsis in English of what was happening. I may have gotten the facts, but I know that the real essence of the events escaped me. That inquisitive streak may be responsible for my interest in studying Spanish and in pursuing a career intertwined with the study of languages in addition to English by Americans. Contact with Mexican laborers, an elementary teacher who loved traveling in Mexico, missionary friends who lived and worked for years in South America, and finally a Spanish teacher who captured my interest and motivated me as no one had before—all this pushed me in the same direction. For me, an Iowa farm kid, this was all strange and unusual. But that was more than thirty years ago. Times and realities are changing.

In 1991, more Americans are studying modern languages in our public high schools than ever before—nearly 40 percent. What's more, they are studying an increasing variety of languages in addition to the usual French, German, Latin, and Spanish. Now it's Chinese, Japanese, and some Arabic; and Russian is growing again. One factor is instantaneous communication and the accompanying awareness of our world; but even more than that, it is the accommodation required of each of us, accepting and acting on the reality of our environment. Dealing with diversity has become a necessity of life, whether we talk of international politics, negotiations for foreign business, the retail business in many of our large cities, or simply understanding, appreciating, and getting along with our neighbors down the street. There is diversity at home and the wealth of language and cultural expertise which it provides. There is the push from Europe as it enters into a new era of cooperation in business, education, and all areas of endeavor. These developments have been brought into focus by the predominance of Japan and other Asian countries in the increasingly intense search for clients and markets.

But the essence of my message goes beyond earning a living. Language is integral to every aspect of life, whether it be our day-to-day routine or the enjoyment of leisure, travel, and the arts. We have traditionally thought of the knowledge of *other* languages and cultures as keys that would open doors and provide new opportunities. It is still true. But another important fact is becoming evident. The events which have brought us together, both here and abroad, also sometimes threaten to tear us apart.

Breaking down barriers of language and culture is a necessity and challenge that awaits and confronts each of us. We may pursue a career that utilizes this knowledge on a daily basis. Or we may simply require these insights and this knowledge to go about our lives. One thing is certain: knowledge of another language and culture will enhance your career—and broaden every aspect of your life.

> C. Edward Scebold
> Executive Director
> American Council of Teachers of Foreign Languages

Preface

This book describes dozens of jobs for people who speak a second language. You will learn about jobs in volunteer organizations, teaching English as a foreign language, working in major corporations with overseas offices or in foreign corporations with offices in the United States. Foreign language skills are needed in library and information science, social service, news gathering, public relations and promotion, advertising and sales, medical and technical fields, teaching, travel and tourism, law enforcement, and jobs with the federal government. Translating, interpreting, teaching, and consulting are other career options. In this book, you will meet many successful people and read about how they got where they are and what they like (and don't like) about jobs that require two or more languages.

Do you love to play with English? Do you like to hear the sounds of foreign languages? Are you attracted to people who speak other languages and come from other cultures? Then you may want to find a career that requires foreign language skills. Are you good with words? Do you like solving problems? Would you enjoy figuring out how to help two people who don't speak the same language get together and meet their goals? Are you something of a mimic? Do you enjoy stand-up comedians? In *Mad Magazine* do you like the strip "Spy Vs. Spy?"

If so, you may be interested in the hundreds of jobs available for people who speak and write a foreign language. This book will give you some of the basics of this rapidly expanding field. You will be surprised, perhaps, at how many areas in our modern society require knowledge of a foreign language. You may also be surprised at how many career opportunities there are that combine the use of a foreign language with some other basic skill or talent.

You are probably aware that you are living in an information age, but you may not be aware of just what cultural and linguistic diversity there is in the information that surrounds you. Events of the past thirty years have brought changes in the way people work with each other, both within countries and from one country to another. New awareness of the value of differences in culture and language make today's society rich and exciting. These differences can also be challenging, especially for those who don't have the cultural and language skills to deal with the new environment.

That's where you come in. With your language skills and your knowledge of two cultures, you can help people communicate with each other. You can help people get the things they want and avoid doing things that would be harmful to them. You can work with people and organizations to bring about true understanding.

You don't have to be a linguistic genius or a polyglot to find a good job and have a satisfying career using your second language. And the rewards of using your language skills are many.

A special feeling comes from being able to help people communicate with each other when they don't speak the same language. Knowing a second language and being able to convey information accurately and appropriately in that language can build one's confidence and self-esteem. Knowing another language may also be the key component of an exciting and financially rewarding career.

Some people have a gift. They seem to be able to learn other languages quickly and remember vocabulary words easily. Other people grow up knowing a second language because it was spoken in their home. For these fortunate individuals, career opportunities abound, if they approach their goal with a clear plan using accurate, up-to-date information.

This book is designed to help provide components for such a plan, and current career information for those who are already well along the way to foreign language fluency. This book will also be valuable for beginning foreign language students who recognize the great career potential that having a second language promises. These people recognize that achieving fluency may require considerable effort, but they feel that the rewards are worth it. Whatever your career field or level of fluency, you can probably find ways to use your language skills to advance your career.

Begin with organizations that accept and need volunteers, and moving on to service and sales positions, the book continues onward to opportunities in teaching English as a second language.

Careers in commerce and business require specialized training or experience in those fields, but knowing a foreign language enhances the applicant's attractiveness to employers. Banking, manufacturing, and consulting firms look for individuals with business savvy and human relations skills. Adding a second language and cross-cultural training to those attributes strengthens a resume considerably.

Information and service careers also demand language skills. Careers in library and information science, human services, journalism and mass communication, and health care are covered in chapters 5–8.

People with a yen to see the world, as well as a desire to develop language skill, can find career opportunities in travel and tourism—a growth area in the coming decade.

And there are jobs at home working for the federal and local government or as a translator, interpreter, or teacher.

The next chapter will give you pointers on how to increase the likelihood of landing a job that lets you use your second language.

CHAPTER ONE

Jobs for Foreign Language Aficionados

Some people have a facility for languages while other people struggle valiantly to learn them. The easiest way to learn another language is to live in a home or in a country where that language is being used every day. You hear the same words and phrases so often that eventually they stick.

It doesn't take a genius to learn another language; little kids do just fine. Cantinflas, the Mexican comedian, once told a good joke on the subject by observing that Americans are so intelligent. "I just returned from a visit to New York," he said, "and even *children* were speaking English there!"

Fluency in a foreign language is not only possible; it's increasingly beneficial. The world keeps getting smaller. It used to take a week bouncing around on the Atlantic Ocean to get from New York to Paris. Nowadays, an airplane will get you there in a few hours. Since it is so easy to travel now, many more people are doing it. Businesspeople, people visiting relatives, tourists—they all crowd the roads, railways, and airways. Increased travel means greater opportunity and incentive to learn foreign languages.

Those who do master another language find plenty of chances to use their skill. It makes travel easier and more pleasant. And many people find themselves using foreign language skills closer to home, with neighbors and co-workers. Opportunities to use foreign language skills on the job are everywhere. And there are career rewards for all types of people who want, or need, to use a language other than their native one.

Develop a Plan

Before you go out looking for jobs, however, it is helpful to decide the level of foreign language skill—and skill in understanding how things are done in other cultures—that you are willing to develop. That decision will help you focus on the career choice or employment opportunity that you can realistically achieve. Then, what you'll probably want to do is set short-term goals that put you on track. Aim for a job where your language skills will be an asset. If you speak German, for example, find out about jobs in which knowledge of German will be useful.

According to *Forbes Magazine*, a key to success for promising employees, regardless of where they work, is a genuine desire to learn and communicate, and the self-confidence to make mistakes. Respect for associates' backgrounds also contributes greatly to success. These same qualities also enhance one's ability to learn a foreign language. And fluency in another language, in turn, increases one's communication skills, self-confidence, and appreciation of other languages and cultures. Paul Aron, vice-chairperson emeritus of Daiwa Securities America, is quoted as saying, "English is an international language, but it isn't *the* international language."

Given all the advantages, maybe you'll want to add a strategic language to those you already know. For example, one student, Alan, was raised in the United States in a Spanish-speaking home. This was neat because he learned one language at home and another—English—outside the home. In high school he began studying a third language—Russian—and enjoyed it. In college he majored in engineering but continued to take Russian courses as electives. After completing his engineering requirements, he went to Moscow to study for a semester.

Since he wanted a job that involved a lot of travel to other countries, he parlayed his fluency in three languages to get a job as an industrial engineer with a firm that had contracts in Latin America and the U.S.S.R. Alan was last seen dropping off the scuba equipment he used on weekends in Costa Rica; he was on his way to catch a plane to Siberia. (One suspects that the next time he shows up in the United States his tan will have faded a bit.) All this travel and adventure was made possible because of his interest in languages.

If you enjoy learning from and communicating with people from diverse backgrounds, a career in which you use a second language may be just right for you. Let's look at some of the possibilities, beginning with those of easiest access and moving on to those requiring more training, but which offer prestige and good salaries.

You may have learned a second language at home or at school, but it is obvious that language skill is aided by some kind of systematic training. However you learned another language, you will want to polish it through *study*. Nobody can say for sure which language will help you get a job. Most, if not all, foreign languages have some market value. In the United States, Spanish is rapidly becoming the dominant language in some cities and a strong factor in communities all over the country. French, German, Portuguese, Italian, Japanese, Chinese, Vietnamese, and Korean are helpful in certain positions. With changes in Eastern Europe and the Soviet Union, languages from those areas will be in demand as economic, social, and political interaction increases. Events in the Mideast and immigration from Southeast Asia are likely to stimulate need for workers who are fluent in languages from those regions.

Volunteer

Organizations of all kinds these days have connections and activities that spill across borders and across oceans. Civic, fraternal, educational, sports, professional, volunteer groups—all need secretaries and other clerical workers who know at least one language in addition to English. If you have clerical and organizational skills, and the basics of a second language, you can find immediate opportunities to use both.

You may have to volunteer your services to get your foot in the door. However, it will be worth volunteering if you improve your language skills and your understanding of organizations that have international connections. The chance to use your language skills, no matter how limited or undeveloped you may feel they are, is vital. You should recognize that being able to say a few words in your target language, or being able to recognize a few words written in another language, is a skill. And speaking a language is like playing a musical instrument: Practice is the key.

Improve Your Skills

Opportunities to improve upon those skills are literally in the air itself. If you can't do anything else, you can listen to shortwave broadcasts in virtually any language you may want to learn. Investment in an inexpensive shortwave radio could be a very positive first step toward increasing your foreign language competence and entering an exciting, rewarding career.

You might also want to tune in to educational or Spanish-language stations on television. Educational stations sometimes air foreign language courses as part of their combined effort with

local community colleges and universities. You can usually receive credit for these courses if you contact the school and
formally enroll. And you may be able to enhance your language
skill by watching a movie or soap opera in another language.
Here's a chance to listen to native speakers of your target language without ever leaving your house. Because Spanish is becoming such a common language in larger cities of the United
States, there is often a Spanish-language station that you can use
as a learning tool.

Other opportunities to improve your language skills can be
found in every middle sized to large city in America and, indeed,
in virtually every town and hamlet as well. Just look at how many
different languages are spoken in our own communities. In
American cities, the number of languages spoken other than
English often tops a hundred. Between recent immigrants and
the many Americans who have foreign-born parents and grandparents, the chance that there's someone who speaks your target
language in your area is great. It takes some (but not much) effort
to find those people, and it takes some self-confidence to approach them, but those are the very skills that you will want to
develop for your career.

You should have a plan. How are you going to develop the
skills that you need to succeed in a career using a foreign language? You may wish to start by getting a realistic picture of the
situation you are in now, and the resources you have at hand.
You already know a little or a lot of some language other than
English. How can you improve your chances of using this skill to
get a job? How can you improve your language skills? Do you
have the funds to take language classes? Can you spend time with
people who speak the language?

It doesn't matter what plan you have, as much as it matters
that you *have* a plan. The plan should be logical, workable, and
should take you from where you are to where you want to be
in manageable steps. Your plan should consist of steps that
include using the tools you have to obtain the skills you need.

Three Keys to Success

Your chances for success will increase if you use three basic concepts as part of your career strategy: attitude, opportunity, and effort.

Attitude

Paul H. Dunn, speaker and author, tells of going to a cafe in a small town. He asked the waitress what he should order for lunch.

She said, "Why don't you try our Enthusiastic Stew?"

"Why do you call it, 'Enthusiastic Stew?'" Dunn asked.

"Because we put everything we've got into it," replied the waitress.

Succeeding in a career that uses your second language skills will require your enthusiasm. Enthusiasm is a way of looking at life. Steve Covey, in his book *Seven Habits of Highly Effective People* (Simon and Schuster, 1989), suggests that success comes to people who are proactive. That means they take action, rather that just responding to what happens to them. And they see things that happen to them as opportunities, even when such incidents appear to be negative. In your career plan, you should include an "attitude checker" that you turn on often to see if your thinking and attitudes are in line with your goals and aspirations. We all get discouraged sometimes, but maintaining a positive, proactive attitude is one key to success.

There is no perfect "type" of person who can succeed in fields where foreign languages are useful or required. Your personality can be whimsical, plodding, analytical. What you need to do is build an attitude that will capitalize on your traits and make them work for you.

Opportunity

The Amazon River is one of the largest in the world. When it reaches the sea in eastern Brazil, the fresh water from the Amazon flows far out into the ocean, beyond the sight of land. The story, probably apocryphal, is told of a sailing ship becalmed off the Brazilian coast. The crew was dying of thirst. They signaled another ship, becalmed in the distance.

"Send us water."

"Let down your buckets where you are," came the signal from the other ship.

"Send us water."

"Let down your buckets where you are."

The thirsty sailors knew it would be fatal to drink sea water, but they did as they were told. They let down the buckets, and to their amazement and joy, the buckets came up filled with fresh water. The ship, though out of sight of land, had sailed into a patch of fresh water that the Amazon River had thrust out into the ocean.

Your career will prosper as you recognize the opportunities to further enhance and develop your second (or third) language skills. These opportunities flourish all around you. You simply have to let down your bucket.

Effort

As you prepare your plan, and begin to build your career, be aware that you are the person who will set the level of the career achievement you wish to attain. It's a good idea to look at all goals as worthwhile. There are no "good" or "bad" goals as you move forward. There are no "high" or "low" goals. There are just goals. There are jobs and career opportunities that require little more effort than showing up for work and having a good attitude. There are career opportunities that require years of training, practice, and the development of specialized skills. The monetary rewards for the latter are usually higher than for the former. But you shouldn't consider only the prestige factors or the monetary rewards. As you make your career plan, think of what will make you happy, and then evaluate how much effort it will take to achieve that goal. Plan to make the reward you want match the amount of effort you are willing and able to put into it.

There are two great books that can help you develop strategies for getting a job abroad:

Krannich, Ronald L. and Caryl R. Krannich, *The Complete Guide to International Jobs and Careers*. Woodbridge, VA: Impact Publications, 1990.

Schuman, Howard, *Making It Abroad*. New York: John Wiley & Sons, 1988.

CHAPTER TWO

Volunteer and Service Occupations

Yael had just graduated form college with a major in international relations. She was born and raised in New York City and spoke English, Hebrew, and Spanish. She wanted to get a job where she could use her Spanish in some international context. But all jobs were hard to get that season, and her fluency in Spanish was mostly derived from book learning. She wondered how to enhance her resume (it doesn't look good to be out of a job too long) and increase her Spanish fluency while she looked for an appropriate job.

Yael found a solution. She volunteered her services to a nonprofit agency that offered social services in a city neighborhood that was populated predominantly by Hispanics. Mostly, during the course of a volunteer day, she heard and spoke Spanish. She added a description of her volunteer work to her resume. Meanwhile, through contacts at this agency, she got ideas for other places where she might want to work. After five months as a volunteer, the agency offered her a paid half-time job. Yael held this position until she landed a full-time job with an international agency with projects in Latin America.

Yael's two short-term goals were realized by her volunteer work. First, she was able to list on her resume a current position in the Hispanic agency. (It's easier to get a job if you already have a job.) And, through using Spanish every day at work, her fluency improved markedly.

Does your career plan call for you to increase your language and crosscultural skills before you enter the international job market, or before you apply for a job that requires more foreign language skills than you currently have? If so, you may want to volunteer your services to one of the many community organizations or programs that work with people who speak your target language. They may need someone to help with correspondence, with answering the telephone, with translations, with grassroots organizing, writing newsletters, doing research, or fund-raising. Sometimes these positions pay a stipend.

Volunteer Organizations

Volunteer organizations might include religious, government, or civic groups. The rest of this chapter is devoted to brief descriptions of these organizations.

Religious Organizations

Many religious organizations have relief programs and missionary programs that function overseas. Local congregations, even small towns, often have direct contact with people who live in other countries and speak other languages.

Many churches offer programs in their own communities for people who have immigrated to the United States. You might want to help in networking activities that help people find assistance for a wide range of problems. You may want to offer to teach classes for these immigrants.

These volunteer tasks will give you many opportunities to use your second language and learn about the target culture. Practice oils the tongue; it takes the squeak out of the voice, removes your hesitancy when dealing with people from other cultures. Most congregations welcome your support and cooperation even if you aren't a member of the congregation. Typically, Christian church groups seek Christian volunteers of any denomination. There are exceptions, however. Jean, a high school student and professed atheist, was welcomed by the local Catholic priest to teach cooking skills to Hmong refugees. All profited from this exchange.

Government Programs

The Peace Corps employs more than 6,000 volunteers, all of whom must be trained in the language of the country to which they are assigned. This is a great program. Since it began in 1961, over 125,000 Americans have worked abroad with the Peace Corps. Returning Peace Corps volunteers have found jobs in all kinds of agencies where knowledge of a foreign language and culture are valued. Your chances of getting accepted into the Peace Corps are much better if you have a skill that is needed by the participating countries. The Peace Corps looks for a wide range of skills in volunteers: engineering, medical, and teaching skills are always appreciated. The Peace Corps provides a great opportunity to learn and improve your foreign language skills.

If you would prefer to volunteer in the United States, you may want to consider VISTA. VISTA is the domestic counterpart of the Peace Corps. They seek volunteers who know Spanish, French, or Indian languages.

The Office of Economic Opportunity also requires language skills for employees. They sponsor community action programs, such as Head Start, as well as legal services, health centers, and programs for migrant workers.

Civic Organizations

There are scores of organizations that have as one of their main functions interaction with people and organizations overseas. Many organizations carry out local programs with specific countries and areas of the world. And different organizations in town may be working with different countries. So, in all likelihood, there is a club, fraternal organization, people-to-people program, or other group that is involved with local people or people overseas who speak your target language. Again, these organizations welcome efforts by members and nonmembers alike who wish to help. Some organizations provide stipends or scholarships to study or live abroad. Such organizations include Rotary Club, People-to-People, Amnesty International, Partners of the Americas, Lions Clubs, Kiwanis, and Sertoma. All are interested in promoting international understanding.

U.S. Civic Groups

Other U.S. voluntary service organizations are less well known. Here is a partial list.

ACORN
300 Flatbush Avenue
Brooklyn, NY 11217

Volunteers must commit to serving for one year, and they receive a salary. ACORN prefers English-speaking applicants who also speak Spanish and who have prior experience in grassroots organizing. Work involves organizing low-income communities around issues such as housing, education, and health.

Los Niños
1300 Continental Street
San Ysidro, CA 92073

This group focuses on community development and needs volunteers who can commit to one year. Program areas are school teaching, nutrition, family gardens, and literacy.

Proyecto Libertad
306 East Jackson, 3rd Floor
Harlingen, TX 78551

The project seeks Spanish-speaking volunteers who have a knowledge of Central American politics to work with Central American refugees in detention centers.

Sioux Indian YMCAs
P.O. Box 218
Dupree, SD 57632

They need volunteers with camp and/or community development skills to live in small, isolated Sioux communities and work on community development projects for between four and ten weeks.

United Farm Workers
P.O. Box 62
La Paz, Keene, CA 93570

They look for volunteers who can spend one year in rural or urban areas organizing farm workers or consumers.

And there are many, many others. Some groups, like the five just mentioned, focus their efforts on people in the United States, many of whom speak little English. Other organizations focus on other countries, especially Third World countries. Some examples of these groups follow.

Volunteering Abroad

American Friends Service Committee
1501 Cherry Street
Philadelphia, PA 19102

They cosponsor six-to-eight-week summer projects involving construction, gardening, arts and crafts, and child care. Fluency in Spanish is usually required.

Amigos de las Américas
5618 Star Lane
Houston, TX 77057

The group seeks volunteers with at least one year of high school Spanish to work in health clinics in Latin America.

Brethern Volunteer Services
451 Dundee Avenue
Elgin, IL 60120

They sponsor a wide range of community development projects in Latin America, the Caribbean, the Middle East, Europe, and China. Most tours are for between one and two years.

Concern/America
P.O. Box 1790
Santa Ana, CA 92702

Hunger-relief and health programs in Bangladesh, Mexico, Central America, Sierra Leone, and the Sudan are the focus. The group seeks volunteers with a degree in public health, nutrition, agriculture, engineering, or medicine. Placements are for a minimum of one year.

Father Wasson's Orphans (Nuestros Pequeños Hermanos)
P.O. Box 1027
Yarnell, AZ 85362

The group has orphanages in Mexico, Haiti, and Honduras. They need volunteers in construction, food preparation, and dorm directors. Placements are for one year. Room and board are provided.

International Voluntary Services
1424 16th Street, N.W., Suite 204
Washington, D.C. 20036

The group sponsors projects in rural development (agriculture, public health, small enterprise, cooperative development, organizational management) in Bangladesh and in several Latin American and African countries. Placement is from two to three years. Room, board, and travel expenses are provided.

Operation Crossroads Africa
475 Riverside Drive
New York, N.Y. 10011

This organization operates self-help projects in community development. Knowledge of French is required for some assignments.

World Teach
Phillips Brooks House
Harvard University
Cambridge MA 02138

This program sends college graduates to Africa, Costa Rica, China, Thailand, Poland, and other countries to teach for one year (usually in English) in secondary school. It cost volunteers about $3,500, but they earn a monthly salary of around $100 per month.

NOTE: Most of these organizations operate with extremely low overhead. When requesting information of these agencies, it is a good idea to enclose a few dollars to help cover mailing expenses.

For More Information

Some excellent sources of more detailed information on these agencies are listed below.

Connections: A Directory of Lay Volunteer Service Opportunities
St. Vincent Pallotti Center
715 Monroe Street, N.E.
Washington, D.C. 20017

Community Jobs
1516 P Street, N.W.
Washington, D.C. 20005

International Directory for Youth Internships
Learning Resources in International Studies
777 United Nations Plaza
New York, N.Y. 10017

International Workcamp Directory
VFP International Workcamps
43 Tiffany Road
Belmont, VT 05730

Invest Yourself
Commission on Voluntary Service and Action
475 Riverside Drive, Room 665
New York, N.Y. 10027

Overseas List: Opportunities for Living and Working in Developing Countries
Augsburg Publishing House
426 Fifth Street
Box 1209
Minneapolis, MN 55440

U.S. Nonprofit Organizations in Development Assistance Abroad
ACVAFS
200 Park Avenue South
New York, N.Y. 10003

Volunteer!: The Comprehensive Guide to Voluntary Service in the U.S. and Abroad
Commission on Voluntary Service and Action
P.O. Box 347
Newton, KS 67114

Work, Study, Travel Abroad: The Whole World Handbook
St Martin's Press
Council on International Educational Exchange
205 East 42nd Street
New York, N.Y. 10017

A Word of Advice About Volunteering

You are following your plan to develop your language skills and launch yourself into an interesting, fruitful career. It is good to remember your overall goal at all times. It is also important to set short-term goals and to undertake activities that will help make your long-term goals successful. To do that, you must really be interested in the people and projects of the organization where you work.

Remember to put the organization's purpose high on your list of priorities. If you approach volunteerism with a selfish attitude and think "I'll do this because I can see how it will help me. But I won't do that because that won't help me," you will probably not be successful. Think it through. Learn to accept assignments enthusiastically. Look for what is needed and begin to do those things that will help your group or organization succeed.

Rebecca had always been interested in Ethiopia. She hadn't had the chance to learn Amharic or any of the other languages spoken there, but she was willing to try. She noticed that there were lots of Ethiopian restaurants in a nearby city. After asking some questions of the people who ran several of the restaurants, Rebecca volunteered to be an aide in a preschool program that catered to Ethiopian children while their parents worked. After a year she had become functional in Amharic just from hearing it all day long from the children and their teachers. She was then invited to continue—as a paid aide.

Volunteering is an excellent way to improve your fluency and job experience, but you should choose an organization whose mission is truly important to you.

CHAPTER THREE

Teaching English as a Second Language

*I*n communities all over the country, new immigrants arrive to work and raise their families, just as our own parents or grandparents did. This continuing stream of immigration stimulates our economy and creates many opportunities for those who can teach English to speakers of other languages.

If you think you would enjoy teaching English as a second language, several options are open to you. Public and private schools at all levels need teachers. Businesses and community groups seek ESL teachers to help adults gain fluency in English. There are English language institutes, American schools abroad, and opportunities to tutor students privately. Whether you want to work with preschoolers or senior citizens, in the United States or abroad, there are always opportunities to teach English as a second language.

Preschool, Primary, and Secondary Schools

Our public and private schools often provide classes in English as a second language (ESL) to students who have not yet developed sufficient fluency in English. This is a school's most common response to students who are just learning English. Many schools go even further. They offer bilingual education, teaching subject matter in the student's native language (so the student won't fall behind in science, math, and social studies) while also teaching English as a second language. Reading and writing skills are often taught in both languages.

Community Colleges and Universities

Most colleges like to have foreign students matriculate for two reasons. First, they enrich the campus social and cultural life, providing American students with broadening experiences of other cultures and peoples. Second, foreign students are a substantial source of income for the colleges. Foreign students generally have to pass an English language proficiency test (TOEFL—Test of English as a Foreign Language) before they are admitted to a degree program. Since many students arrive without the required level of English fluency, many colleges offer special intensive programs in English for these students so they can do well academically and participate fully in the life of the college. At the least, ESL courses are offered for foreign students.

Survival English

Adults in the community who are learning English as a second (or third) language have immediate needs that must be met quickly. Learning enough English to survive in the United States is one of the most important of those needs. Survival requires being able to communicate in emergencies to police, fire-fighters, health workers, school administrators. It means filling out a job application and being able to read safety signs at the workplace. Survival requires skill in buying food at the supermarket, in using public transportation, or in getting a driver's license. For some immigrants, basic literacy is an immediate need.

These are the kinds of issues that ESL teachers focus on while teaching adults. These ESL classes are generally offered in the evenings. They provide a part-time source of income to the ESL teacher. The vast majority of these teachers find the work exceptionally rewarding. It is fun to teach English to motivated adults from other lands. One Los Angeles ESL teacher put it this way: "These are special people, and they capture your heart."

English for the Workplace

The level of education for an average immigrant is several years higher than for Americans in general. Still, many immigrants arrive with only a few years of primary education. Immigrants without marketable technical skills, or well-educated immigrants lacking English skills, often find work in food service at restaurants of hotels. They may find jobs as taxi drivers or housekeepers. Wherever the work, learning English is usually an advantage.

Sometimes a corporation will offer ESL classes to its employees. These classes develop skill in using the kind of English that the workers need. Construction workers learn a different set of vocabulary from cab drivers. These ESL courses benefit both business and employees, and they may provide the perfect teaching opportunity for you.

English has become the international language of many professions: airline pilots and air controllers, business-people and diplomats. In many fields of study, especially technical areas, the only available textbooks are written in English. The result is that there are many people in the United States and other countries of the world who would like to learn some English to pursue their profession. This provides work opportunities for you if you would like to teach ESL, either in the United States or abroad.

American Schools Abroad

Most private schools abroad teach students English. Even American schools enroll students who are just learning English. The American School in Guatemala, for example, enrolls about 15 percent Americans; the rest are mostly Guatemalans. Of the eighty-five percent who are nonnative speakers of English, many are struggling with English. American schools abroad need dynamic people with experience teaching ESL. The schools generally require a teaching certificate from some state in the United States.

Investigating these teaching opportunities may be easier than you would think. Knowing that few schools will hire a teacher without a personal interview, one experienced teacher stopped by the local American schools of each country she visited while on a tour of Europe. Sure enough, she landed a job.

English Language Institutes

Every urban area of the world has privately run language schools, and English inevitably is one of the languages offered. Frequently, American tourists looking to prolong their stay in an interesting port of call will drop by these establishments and inquire into the possibility of employment. Usually the openings are for part-time teachers, and the pay is modest—barely enough to live on, if your needs are simple. But this is a wonderful way for you to meet people and get better acquainted with the country, and to help pay for the experience.

The U.S. Information Service, associated with U.S. embassies abroad, often maintains binational culture centers in major cities. These centers feature libraries of English books, cultural events (plays, art exhibitions, lectures), and—most importantly—classes in English as a second language. Bruce had always wanted to spend a few years in Greece, and prior to visiting

Greece, he wrote to the director of the binational center there, enclosing a resume and indicating that he would be in the country for a visit on a set date and would call to arrange a meeting. Bruce not only got a job as ESL teacher, but things worked out so well that he became the center's director of curriculum several years later.

Private Tutoring

Often people who can afford to will hire a tutor to teach them, or their family, English. They find tutoring is a convenient way to learn the language. The tutor often goes to the student's home and teaches for an hour or two at a time, once or more a week. In some countries, this can provide a reasonable living for the ESL teacher. One ESL teacher in Tokyo, for example, has been teaching the same family English for 20 years! One gets these jobs by advertising and through personal contacts.

Qualifications

Wherever you work, employers look for two major qualifications in ESL teachers. The first requirement is training in the techniques of teaching English to speakers of other languages. The other qualification is actual experience in teaching English as a second language. Both are important to your success as an ESL teacher.

Naturally, the more training you have, the more marketable you become. Some jobs, like those in colleges, generally require a graduate degree in ESL, sometimes a Ph.D. The jobs in public primary and secondary schools usually require state teacher certification. It is still possible, however, for someone with just a bachelor's degree to land a job as an ESL teacher. And jobs as teachers' aides generally do not require more than a high school education.

Often two or three years of experience teaching ESL are sought by prospective employers. This creates the classic dilemma: How do you get experience if employers want people who already have experience? As the singer Ray Charles puts it in one of his songs, "How you get the first is still a mystery to me." You can meet the Catch-22 requirement for prior experience in several ways. Consider starting as a volunteer in a private agency's program (see chapter 2), or work as a teacher aide, or plan to graduate from a program that includes a teaching practicum. John, an English major who enjoyed working with people from other cultures, wanted to learn Russian, but his college didn't offer it. During summer break at the end of his junior year in college, John made arrangements to work for room and board as an ESL teacher's aide in a summer program in the U.S.S.R., gaining the chance to learn the language and experience the culture.

In addition to teaching experience and knowledge of ESL methods, sometimes two other qualifications are sought. They are knowledge of a foreign language and experience living in a second culture.

ESL teachers can anticipate the specific problems that their students will experience if the teachers know the students' native language. For instance, if the student speaks Spanish, the teacher knows that the American "r" sound, and the "th" and light "i" sounds, will give the student some trouble. Sometimes it is not practical to speak the student's language because there may be twenty different languages represented in one classroom. Even so, to have experienced themselves the process of learning a foreign language helps teachers understand the students' problems.

Experience living in another culture is also helpful for ESL teachers. It improves a teacher's accent and increases fluency to use the language on a daily basis with native speakers. And knowledge of another culture can help the ESL teacher educate and understand students better. In addition, assignments abroad are easier to land if the employer knows that the teacher is comfortable living in other countries and enjoys experiencing a new culture.

For More Information

Sources of information on careers in teaching English as a second language are listed below.

Association of Teachers of English as a Second Language
National Association for Foreign Student Affairs (NAFSA)
1860 19th Street, N.W.
Washington, D.C. 20009

Center for Applied Linguistics
1118 22nd Street, N.W.
Washington, D.C. 20037

Institute of International Education
809 United Nations Plaza
New York, NY 10017

International Schools Service
P.O. Box 5910
Princeton, NJ 93944

TESOL (Teachers of English to Speakers of Other Languages)
1600 Cameron Street
Alexandria, VA 22314
(Most states and many foreign countries have affiliates.)

Worldwide Employment Services
10 East 39th Street, Suite 910
New York, NY 10016
(There is a substantial registration fee.)

CHAPTER FOUR

Commerce and Business

New technology links the world as never before. Our planet has shrunk. It's now a "global village" where countries are only seconds away by fax or phone or satellite link. Teleconferencing, portable satellite links, radio telephones, and other high-tech advances make foreign markets as close as our crosstown branch office. And, of course, our ability to benefit from this high-tech communication equipment is greatly enhanced by foreign language skills.

Deeply involved with this new technology is a breed of modern business-people who have a growing respect for the economic value of doing business abroad. In modern markets, success overseas often helps support and revitalize domestic business efforts.

Overseas assignments are becoming increasingly important to advancement within executive ranks. The executive stationed in another country no longer need fear being "out of sight and out of mind." He or she can be sure that the overseas effort is central to the company's plan for success, and that promotions often follow or accompany an assignment abroad. If an employee can succeed in a difficult assignment overseas, superiors will have greater confidence in his or her ability to cope back in the United States where cross-cultural considerations and foreign language issues are becoming more and more prevalent.

Thanks to a variety of relatively inexpensive communications devices with business applications, even small businesses in the United States are able to get into markets where the medium of exchange is the mark, the yen, the peso, or the pound. Large corporations have international branches or divisions, and they deal with foreign investors and buyers on a daily basis. English is still the international language of business. The American dollar still talks clearly in the world marketplace. But there is an ever-growing need for people who can decipher another tongue. A second language isn't generally required to get a job in business, but having language skills gives a candidate the edge when other qualifications appear to be equal.

The employee posted abroad who speaks the country's principal language has an opportunity to fast-forward certain negotiations, and can have the cultural insight to know when it is better to move more slowly. The employee at the home office who can communicate well with foreign clients over the telephone or by fax machine is an obvious asset to the firm. Such persons build a niche for themselves in the firm. They find themselves included in the "loop" in which key company business is discussed.

Important Languages

According to a job service based in San Francisco, the leading languages that will be vital to U.S. business success in the next two decades are Spanish, first, then Japanese, then French, Chinese, German, and Russian. This research was carried out before dramatic political and economic changes took place in Eastern Europe.

Even more languages can be included in the list, and the order may be different depending on what business you are in. There are about twenty "industrialized" nations. These include Poland, Sweden, and Italy. Knowledge of Polish, Swedish, or Italian can be a real advantage to a businessperson.

Industrialized nations do not trade exclusively with other industrialized nations. They also trade with "Third World nations," lesser developed countries in Africa, Asia, and Latin America that nevertheless buy products from more economically developed countries. And, of course, it is easier to sell something to someone if you speak his or her language. Forcing the client to speak a foreign language in order to place an order with you puts you at a distinct disadvantage.

Asian languages are also vital to the new economic mix. The United States imports billions of dollars of merchandise annually from Taiwan, Korea, China, and Japan. And the entrepreneur with Russian or German or Chinese language skills—or the corporation with employees fluent in those languages—has a better chance than most of taking advantage of the developing business opportunities in those parts of the world.

With so many choices, which languages should you study to advance your business career? Of course, the answer depends on your individual interests and aspirations. However, Spanish rates as the second language of the world, and, if you are looking for a career language that has high potential, Spanish may be it. Spanish can be easier to learn than some other languages because Spanish classes are offered in virtually every U.S. town, and you can easily find native speakers of Spanish to converse with. Demographic projections show that the percentage of native Spanish-language speakers will increase dramatically in the next two decades in the United States. With that rise in Spanish speakers will come an increase in the need for people who speak both English and Spanish and are comfortable with cultural realities of both societies.

Teaching Languages to Businesspeople

Business schools have begun to integrate foreign language requirements into their programs as they recognize the importance of language skills to their graduates' success "in the outside world." Some companies take the position that it is easier to teach a good businessperson a second language than it is to teach a language-skilled individual how to succeed in business. That fact in itself offers career opportunities. Jobs and business opportunities are available for people who know other languages and can teach them effectively to business school students and business executives who travel abroad.

Setting aside for the moment the language programs of universities and colleges, there are many organizations that teach "intensive" language courses on a commercial basis. Some of these courses consist of ten 1-hour sessions. The students learn grammar, usage, and cultural skills. Such organizations offer jobs and career opportunities for teachers, office personnel, and curriculum specialists who recognize the importance of cross-cultural understanding and nonverbal nuances in communicating with students.

Culture camps and workshops are another offshoot of the growing need for knowledge of foreign languages in commerce and industry. Language "cramming" is only part of the curriculum and of culture camps. Other elements included are etiquette of the target society, and "do's and don'ts." This training makes it easier to move into target cultures without making a serious faux pas. Jobs at culture camps would be similar to those in language schools, but the camps put special emphasis on foreign cultural practices.

Job List

Following is a list of jobs in banking, manufacturing, consulting firms, and multinational corporations. Some of these positions require knowledge of a foreign language, but most do not. Even though the words "second language required" currently appear on relatively few business and industrial job descriptions, the realities of the business world already discussed strongly imply a need for language skills. It is up to you to take advantage of these implications and reinforce them through your own efforts to land a position or prepare for a career using your language skills.

You should also note that this list is by no means inclusive. For every industry, and for virtually every company, there are infinite variations of requirements and expectations. Even in jobs requiring the most basic skills, the ability to communicate well can be the key to advancement.

Computers

Everything we deal with these days is computerized—cars, television sets, microwave ovens, wristwatches, cash registers. The list is almost endless. The United States exports computers, computer software, and computer components. Thus language skills are used in these positions:

systems consultant

programmer

troubleshooter and repair person

installer

operator

hard data librarian

Banking

Banking is the grandfather of international commerce. Banking executives and bank employees play well-established and long-standing roles in the field. What is new is the amount of bilingual and multicultural business coming into routine banking activities and procedures. In the following positions language skills can prove valuable:

bank president

teller

receptionist

investment counselor

vice-president

loan officer

Advertising

The U.S. advertising business was hard hit by the recession of the late eighties and early nineties. Advertising growth was almost flat as U.S. firms adjusted their budgets. A number of advertising firms were able to expand their overseas clientele at a time when national account activity was sluggish. Opportunities in advertising will be more fully discussed in Chapter 7. But for purposes of this business chapter, advertising positions break down into the following major areas:

public relations practitioner

billboard and graphic designer

account executive

marketing specialist

electronic media specialist

sales executive

publicity and in-house promotion person

Personnel

Whether in the United States or in the foreign division of a multinational corporation, personnel departments play a role of importance. Coordinating the needs and expectations of the company and the employees helps move the company forward. Following are personnel positions that are increasingly being filled by language qualified people:

employee relations adviser

employee insurance adviser

personnel officer

systems trainer

grievance facilitator

research coordinator

Customer Service

All businesses depend on customer service employees who can deal with requests of all kinds, and take care of all kinds of problems with speed, accuracy, and diplomacy. Foreign language skills are always an asset in these jobs. Following are positions in customer service:

receptionist

cash register operator

service and repair person

customer greeter

service desk person

salesperson

delivery person

public relations specialist

The lists in this chapter break the surface of jobs available in business for people with language skills. Banking, retail, manufacturing, and advertising are all going multinational and will all require second languages of their employees in the years to come. For every position mentioned, a dozen more exist or could be created. And while knowledge of a second language may not be a prerequisite to employment, having a foreign language can make you stand above a group of monolingual job applicants. The best advice in the business area is to get a specific skill that you are interested in following as a career, and take steps to learn a language that will enhance your value to the company.

The best strategy usually calls for getting a job with a U.S. firm that does business abroad, then positioning yourself within the company for an overseas assignment. That way you get paid in dollars at what is usually a higher salary rate than that paid for comparable jobs in the host country.

Library and Information Science

W e live in the Information Age. The depth and breadth of human knowledge is expanding at an amazing rate. So much new information is produced around the world each day that it is impossible to keep track of it all. Information is power. Those with the technical and artistic skills to sift through this glut of data and extract the relevant tidbits required by a client or employer are increasingly rare finds and, therefore, are more and more valuable to many employers. This is the expertise of the librarian and the information researcher.

Libraries exist in all parts and levels of our society and go by many names: media centers, electronic data bases, archives, and information centers. A library by any other name is still a library: a storehouse of information. This information can be stored in many formats that go beyond the traditional bound book. Electronic storage utilizing computer technology is becoming more popular, convenient, and efficient.

The usefulness of multiple language skills will depend on the type of library where you work and your job title. There are basically four types: public libraries, school libraries, research libraries, and special or corporate libraries. The particular language skills required will also depend upon what specific area you work in within the library organization.

Types of Libraries

Understanding your attitudes toward your work environment is very important when considering a job in library service. Library types are defined by the community that they are designed to serve. Corporate and research libraries are highly structured, and the information needs of their users are often very technical and demanding. The parameters often are highly specific and detailed, and often come with deadlines and cost restraints attached. School and public libraries, on the other hand, are far less demanding of technical skills but will require a more people-centered approach.

In all types of libraries and all facets of the job, computers are playing a larger role. Anyone contemplating a career in library service or information science needs to be comfortable with computers and other technologies. Because of the rapid advances and upgrades in this industry, you must also be adaptable and trainable. A technical understanding of computers is not necessary, just a familiarity with computer applications and a willingness to learn more. Within the library profession, there are ample opportunities for both technically minded and people-oriented personalities.

How your language skills will help you, and what expertise is required on the job, will be more precisely determined by the area of the library you work in, by the opportunities that arise, and by the effort you expend.

Training

Whatever job you perform in the library world, it is important to get training in library skills and information management. On the job is a good place to start, to see if you like the work and to acquire basic knowledge. Many colleges and universities offer elective courses in library use and bibliographic instruction that would be very valuable. High-level jobs and employment at research libraries generally will require a master's degree in library and information science.

All library jobs fall into one of two categories: patron services or technical services. Those in the first category work directly with the community. The key responsibility here is reference service.

Patron Services

Reference librarians deal directly with the library users and help patrons locate the information they desire. In public and school libraries, this requires good human relations skills. Technical perfection in a second language is not as important as being open to foreign language patrons at the library and understanding their needs. Certainly basic conversational skills are paramount. And developing basic reading skills in another language enables a librarian to find the appropriate book or magazine for a patron—even if the vocabulary of the material itself is beyond the librarian's capabilities. Here, too, a feeling for the culture beyond words and verb conjugations is a valuable asset.

Many libraries seek to expand their offerings to include titles in the native languages of their clients. Chris, a librarian in an inner-city grade school, calls Spanish-speaking people in the area for leads on books written in Spanish that children enjoy. She also attends book fairs to get ideas and occasionally visits a Spanish-speaking country on a book-buying tour.

Library administrators are looking for confident, open employees to staff their reference department—employees who are comfortable with people regardless of their ethnic or language background. If you are a "people person" who is willing to use your language skills—however halting and rudimentary—to communicate with patrons and successfully help them find the library materials they seek, you will be a valuable addition to a public or school library staff.

Reference work at a research or corporate/special library requires a much greater fluency in foreign languages and higher level library-searching skills. Where the information sought at a public library may consist of a good book or a consumer report on used car quality, the information needs at research and special libraries are usually far more technical and exacting. A broad vocabulary in all your acquired languages is a must in order to understand patron queries and provide accurate answers.

If working in reference or in special libraries interests you, plan on extensive educational preparation. In university research libraries, it is routine to require one or even two foreign language proficiencies for a reference position. In addition, an advanced degree in library science and a college degree in the specific subject within which you will work is required. Your undergraduate work should include developing an understanding of the technical vocabulary within your subject specialty.

Your chosen subject specialty will often dictate the language proficiency that would be most useful. Any foreign language fluency can be useful, but for some specialties certain languages are more helpful than others. For example, if you have a bachelor's degree in chemistry and wish to work as a science or reference librarian, German, Russian, and Japanese would be more useful to you than Polish or Portuguese. If you work in literature or economics, Spanish, French, or Chinese might be more applicable than Bahasa Indonesian. On the other hand, if the library caters to a community of Portuguese- or Indonesian-speaking people, then this would not be true.

Because reference librarians at these larger or more specialized libraries can also be asked to translate material for patrons, the most advanced language proficiencies can make you very useful and valuable. Translating articles or technical manuals within a research discipline requires the most fluency and technical skills of any library language assignment.

Technical Services

The second category of library work is technical services. Here, librarians work with the information materials directly—whether they be books, paintings, movies, exhibits, or electronic data. They work to categorize, catalog, and organize the materials to make them readily available and accessible to the community. These jobs do not require the interpersonal communication skills that patron services do. As in reference, different levels of language ability can be useful in the technical services area.

Acquisitions

Acquisition of material is an important technical service. This department selects material for purchase. Prescreening of foreign language material may only require a rudimentary understanding of another language, enough to make the librarian capable of recognizing a good review in a literary publication in that language. When materials arrive in the library, someone must decide what department should receive them. This is not as simple as it might sound, particularly in the case of materials published or produced in a foreign country.

Research libraries, in particular, receive materials from all over the world, and not just materials that support the teaching of foreign languages. In assembling a reliable collection on any subject, there are important contributions made in many languages. When this material arrives at the library, someone needs to identify what language it is in and what subject area it deals with. This could best be done by individuals with a broad familiarity with languages, but neither fluency nor even basic communication skills is needed.

Materials in foreign languages purchased by public or school libraries are not as far ranging. Foreign language needs are dictated by the community the library serves. It is important for employees in both technical and patron services to have language skills that reflect the demographics of the local community. In the United States, the single most important second language for a public or school librarian is Spanish, though obviously in most urban areas there will be concentrations of languages from all over the world, and any second language skill will be valuable in major metropolitan areas.

Cataloging

The second major technical service is cataloging. To be a cataloger in a research or special library requires an advanced degree in library science. This is also where the most language expertise is required in technical services. Catalogers need to be able to identify the key subjects addressed by the material and then accurately describe it both in the language of the library in which it appears and in English or the principal language of the library. This requires a broad vocabulary, and, like reference service researchers, library catalogers usually specialize in one or more subject areas. This means they must have the expanded vocabulary requisite for their specialization. Though technical accuracy is a must, written and verbal communication skills are not necessary. All of a cataloger's job is reading and writing, so proper accents and vocal nuance are unnecessary.

If you are interested in being a part of the Information Age and have a bit of the private eye spirit in you, your second or multilanguage skills can be put to profitable use in library and information science. If you like to find the needle in the haystack, the *Stecknadel* in the *Hauhaufen*, the *aguja* in the *pajar,* and the *tsahts'ósí* in the *tl'oh,* this could be the job for you.

For More Information

For further information on librarianship, write to these associations:

American Library Association
50 East Huron Street
Chicago, IL 60611

Special Libraries Association
1700 18th Street, N.W.
Washington, D.C. 20009

CHAPTER SIX

Human Services

One interesting professional area with employment opportunities for people with language skills is the field of
human services. Like the health care professionals,
human service workers come into contact with people who are
poor, unemployed, victims of child abuse, homeless, or in poor
health. The work settings can be as diverse as group homes and
halfway houses; correctional centers; mental health facilities;
family, child, and youth service agencies; substance abuse programs.

While jobs for social workers do not pay especially well, the
job outlook calls for a faster than average expansion in the
number of jobs available through the year 2000. One area of
growth, for example, is in services to the aged.

Another area of human services is recreational services. Jobs
in the area of recreation are expected to grow about as fast as
those in other areas of the economy. Recognition that in many
areas many clients speak little English will make it easier for
qualified people with language skills to find jobs in the field of
human services.

Another source of jobs is private and government organizations that help immigrants and other people with limited fluency
in English get along in the United States. These groups require

employment counselors, caseworkers, and supervisors who speak the language of their clients. Opportunities for social service careers are not limited to major cities where immigrant populations tend to be large. Many immigrant people live in widely dispersed areas of the country. They are found in all regions and states, in big cities and small towns.

There are positions in social work that involve working with employment records, resumes, legal documents of all kinds, and correspondence with social agencies abroad. This work requires people who are able to decipher foreign languages and tease information out of odd-appearing documents.

Job Requirements and Challenges

As with positions in the health care professions, social work positions tend to be "people intensive." They require you to be interested in helping others with a variety of social needs, from education and employment to individual personal and family matters. If your career plan includes some kind of social work, you will want to study the ways in which language skills and human skills combine in this area. You will, as in the case of volunteers discussed in chapter 2, want to focus your efforts on making things better for your clients.

You will want to familiarize yourself with the regulations and requirements of the social agencies and organizations you represent. You will want to identify potential problems that these regulations and requirements might pose for your clients who speak a language other than English, and who may come from a cultural background different from your own.

Such potential problems may not lie just in the differences in language. If people have religious, dietary, social, or political customs or beliefs that conflict with the regulations of your agency or organization, you may be the only person who can solve the dilemma. And to solve it, you will have to understand the regulations involved as well as the cultural reality that controls your client.

One example of a cultural tradition clashing with the tradition of a social service agency occurred in Chicago as a state agency attempted to provide group health and education counseling to a tribe of Gypsies. The way the agency organized the group sessions offended these Gypsies' sense of propriety. The agency had proposed that the groups be divided into age levels. The Gypsy leaders were horrified that grandchildren were to be separated from their grandparents and equally upset that males and females were to be together in the same class. The counselors in this case proved to be flexible and a simple compromise solution was agreed upon—to divide the classes by sex but not by age. Social service work often demands the ability to make such compromises.

Social Work

Social workers generally help people who are having difficulties dealing with circumstances in their lives. There are many kinds of social workers. The major areas of social work practice include child welfare and family services, mental health, medical social work, school social work, community organization, planning and policy development, and social welfare administration. A bachelor's degree is usually the minimum academic requirement to work in these fields. Often a master's degree is required. A social worker's effectiveness in helping people who do not speak English is mightily aided by a knowledge of the client's native tongue.

Frequently, the needs of someone from a particular country can be anticipated by a knowledge of the client's culture. Many people from India, for instance, are Hindu. Among their religious practices is a proscription against eating meat. Single males need to identify area restaurants where good vegetarian food is served—not just fruit salads.

Community Affairs

Planning

If you have organizational skills, you may want to work with people who plan activities that focus on, or seek participation of, ethnic and linguistic groups in the community. These activities may be anything from a large budget annual observance like "Spanish American Heritage Week," that is put on for the whole community or region, to a picnic for preschool children in a small ethnic neighborhood.

Again, it is difficult to overemphasize the need for knowledge of the cultures involved as well as sensitivity to the social hierarchy of the target community. You may have to check with people about what kind of colors to use in the banners and bunting, what sort of food and drink would be appropriate, as well as giving advice to your superiors on which dates to plan events and which dates to avoid holding certain activities. Your advice on the type and location of sites for the events may also be needed.

Communication

This work involves, among other things, getting the English language mass media—newspapers, magazines, radio, and television—to be aware of, and involved with, the cultural and linguistic groups in your community. It also involves writing, speaking yourself, and identifying individuals in the target community who are good spokespersons.

There are many levels of positions and job opportunities in community affairs planning and community affairs communication. They range all the way from people who work at setting up and carrying out the activities, to people who plan the activities, to people who have overall responsibility for planning and coordinating all cultural and linguistic efforts that the community undertakes.

Sometimes it is difficult to find any long-term residents of a community who speak the language of the most recent residents. There are towns in Minnesota, for example, that have become home to sizable numbers of Hmong immigrants, a mountain tribe of farmers from Vietnam. Making effective contact with them has required identifying a network of human resources in the state that could help inform social workers about Hmong customs, aspirations, and problems. People who could speak Hmong were needed to assist in the initial contacts. One especially successful community affairs planner not only set up a good network of people who could contribute something to the needs of the Hmong; he also made arrangements to have local Hmong tutor him in the language. This was widely appreciated in the Hmong community.

Home Health Aides

Many social services consist of helping people who have had health or emotional problems and now need home visits from time to time to monitor their progress and give them assistance. It is hard to help if you can't understand the client's language. And an appreciation of the person's culture can also help in providing health care.

A sizable community of people from the Dominican Republic reside in a town in New Jersey. With what most temperate-zone Americans would regard as minor changes in temperature, many Dominicans feel a cold coming on. To help them feel comfortable in their new home, one successful home health aide provided them with an orientation that included how to identify cod liver oil and where to buy it. In syrup or pill form, cod liver oil is widely taken in many parts of Latin America as a cough remedy.

For More Information

Further information on job openings in the field of human services may be available from state employment agencies or from city, county, or state departments of health, mental health and mental retardation, and human resources.

For additional information on careers in human service, you may want to contact:

National Organization for Human Service Education
P.O. Box 6257
Fitchburg State College
Fitchburg, MA 01420

Council for Standards in Human Service Education
Montgomery Community College
340 Dekalb Pike
Blue Bell, PA 19422

Journalism and Mass Communication

M ass communication can be broken down into a number of fields under two headings: electronic media and print media. Electronic media include the radio, television, motion picture and music industries, as well as communication industries like telephone, telegraph, satellite, and cable operators. The major print media are books, magazines, and newspapers, but the heading can include pamphlets, flyers, press releases—just about any printed form of information exchange.

Career possibilities in mass communication fields are expanding with the population size. Specialization of programming and content for target audiences has been increasing in recent years, and with it the opportunities for people with second language skills.

Particularly in the United States, the rise of Spanish-language newspapers, magazines, radio broadcasts, and television shows has become pronounced. Many local TV stations produce programming for sections of the viewing audience who speak a primary language other than English. German-language newspapers, Spanish magazines, and Russian radio shows can be heard in places throughout the United States.

Major news networks have bureaus in many foreign venues, with large staffs of reporters, photographers, editors, technicians, and other support people. News work in other countries can be found through a number of communication companies such as ABC, CBS, NBC, CNN, INN, AP, and others. There are dozens of positions that must be filled to make any media company workable.

Print Media

Book Publishing

Thousands of new books are published each year. Take a look at any bookstore and see for yourself. And nearly as many will be translated for markets overseas, or translated into English for the U.S. market. Publishers need a variety of people in a number of positions to read and translate manuscripts. Here are some of the standard jobs in book publishing:

reader

editor

copy editor

typesetter

reviewer

proofreader

designer

printer

promoter

publisher

author

As you can see, the job opportunities in book publishing are diverse. And most require a combination of language skills and some other talent, such as artistic, sales, or writing ability. If publishing interests you, plan to develop both your language skills and another specialization. For example, designers need a background in art, promoters often study marketing. And many publishing professionals take continuing education courses designed specifically for those in the field.

As in all fields, work experience is the best way to test your interest and aptitude. Internships, entry-level jobs, and freelance positions provide great on-the-job training and a good introduction to the world of publishing. You can locate potential employers through the yellow pages or by doing research in sources such as *Literary Marketplace*. Check with your reference librarian for suggestions on getting started.

Magazines

Magazines originally developed from newspapers, but have since nearly swamped the publishing world. Using better paper, more color and photographs, and a different writing style, magazines have constantly evolved to suit the needs and whims of society. Now, specialty magazines cover every conceivable subject, from cats to monster movies, from log homes to modern science. And many specialty magazines have begun to serve the needs of people with a second language. Here are some common positions on a magazine staff.

staff writer

freelance writer

columnist

photographer

layout artist

copy editor

managing editor

editor in chief

publisher

marketing specialist

advertising salesperson

printer

typesetter

Because magazines offer diverse job options and cover a wide range of subjects, you should be able to combine your skills and interests in seeking a job in this field. Jobs for editors and graphic artists are expected to increase at a faster than average rate through the year 2000. Competition for jobs in magazine and book publishing, however, is stiff. That's because so many people are attracted to these jobs. However, skill in a second language can help make you more marketable. You should plan to combine your language skills with other specialized education and as much job experience as you can develop before seeking your first full-time job in publishing. Your chances of finding a job in magazine publishing are also enhanced if you are willing to locate in a major city such as New York or Chicago where more publishers exist.

Newspapers

Many of the jobs at a newspaper are similar to those at a magazine or a publishing house. The main difference between newspaper and magazine work is the styles and substance of writing. Newspapers generally focus on timely newsworthy events, possibly going into depth on a topic over a period of several days of daily publishing. Magazines, by their nature, allow longer deadline periods which lend the writer more time to dig into a story, develop it, and deliver it in a polished form.

Newspapers have access to the worldwide news-gathering capabilities of the Associated Press and the United Press International, as well as foreign news services such as Reuters and Agence France Press. Nevertheless, when important news breaks abroad, newspapers may send their own staff reporters to the scene. This is particularly true when the news event affects the local area directly.

Staff reporters chosen for these short-term overseas assignments are, first, good reporters. Secondly, they are often persons with language or cross-cultural skills. Often the language the reporter speaks may not be the language of the area where the news event is taking place, but local editors often perceive individuals with languages skills as qualified for assignments anywhere abroad.

The U.S. Department of Labor expects an average number of job openings in journalism through the year 2000. Competition for the available jobs in the field is always keen. But the increasing number of small town and suburban papers, combined with the high turnover rate in the industry, will provide new jobs for journalism graduates. And language skills will give you a competitive edge, especially if they are combined with a degree in journalism and experience on your school or local paper.

In addition to using language skills abroad, local reporters may find opportunities to speak their target language while investigating a news story or writing a human interest piece that involves people with little or no fluency in English.

Electronic Media

Radio

Radio has changed dramatically over the years. It began as a medium of the spoken word, became a medium of sophisticated entertainment programs—including comedy, drama, game, and variety shows—then was gradually superseded by the rising star of television.

Formats changed, listeners changed, but radio continues to grow. What car on the road is complete without a radio? What home doesn't have a radio in every bedroom or living room? All oldies, all rock, all gospel, all talk, all news—all these formats are in use and surviving across the nation.

All Spanish stations are common in the western states, and the government still beams foreign-language programming into hundreds of countries, including the Soviet Union. Jobs abound in radio for people with second languages. Although the skill generally is not required for employment, in most cases there are those positions for which a second language is a prerequisite. Here are some of the jobs you could pursue:

disc jockey

advertising salesperson

station manager

reporter

meteorologist

news announcer

producer

program manager

format manager

Like the other communications careers, radio is a popular field. it tends to attract more people than can find employment. So although the Department of Labor expects average job growth through the year 2000, competition for positions at radio stations will be keen. Most find that it is easiest to get a start at smaller stations outside the major metropolitan areas. Pay for these positions can be low, and many aspiring disc jockeys work in small towns for years before getting a chance to go on the air at a larger station.

Television

Television is the instant-communication media of choice world-wide. More people than ever are turning to television to get their news and form their opinions. Hundreds of channels are available over satellite transmission in the United States alone, and hundreds more are beamed from other countries into our airspace. Cable systems join the homes of rural communities with the centers of commerce and government, allowing instant communication of even the most trivial events.

The popularity of television means jobs. The array of jobs in television includes positions like these:

camera operator

sound technician

lighting technician

set designer

director

engineer

electrician

character generator

writer

copy editor

video editor

audio editor

composer

musician

on-air personality

producer

As you would imagine, most of these jobs require specialized skills and training unrelated to foreign language fluency. However, as the number of Spanish-language and educational stations increases, fluency in a second language will be a special asset in this competitive field.

Foreign Correspondents

Some reporters, from both print and electronic media, spend most of their time abroad. Such assignments offer an interesting way to use second-language skills. Sometimes, however, assignments abroad can become *too* interesting, as newsworthy events often occur in dangerous locales. In response to the often sensitive conditions under which journalists work abroad, The American Committee of the International Press Institute has published a book entitled *Journalists on Dangerous Assignments: A Guide for Staying Alive*, edited by Louise Falls Montgomery. In this book, many veteran correspondents offer their suggestions.

Some of the suggestions they offer will give you a flavor of the danger involved in working as a foreign correspondent:

1. Always try to pick up guides who know the township and its personalities. But once in the car, don't let them wave clenched first salutes from the windows in case the police see this as an incitement.

2. Any reporter who climbs into a police armored vehicle to cover the police side of the story in a township would be well

advised not to visit that township again if there is any possibility at all of being recognized.

3. Never put seat belts on while driving in a war zone because you might have to jump from the car quickly to avoid bullets.

4. Never make anyone sit in the back seat of a two-door car because it will be difficult if not impossible to get out quickly.

In the stressful conditions that foreign correspondents often encounter, strong communication skills are a must. Not only are they important for your own comfort and safety, they are an essential part of doing the job well. The correspondent's duty is to report the facts as completely and accurately as possible. In order to do that, a journalist must be able to understand his or her sources, and the subtleties of the language they speak.

In addition, it is helpful for foreign correspondents to attain as much knowledge of and sensitivity to other culture as they can. Such awareness often makes it easier for a journalist to gain the confidence of sources and hosts in another country. Understanding the culture is just part of the job.

The Entertainment Industry

Music, television, movies, and radio are becoming locked into a symbiotic relationship of promoting each other's product, while struggling among themselves for the discriminating consumer's dollar. But competition is healthy, and the cross-pollinating of each other's industrial flowers seems to keep everyone happy.

As the entertainment industry grows, so does the number of entertainers, especially musicians and actors. These entertainers perform in all languages and in every country. If you have musical or dramatic talent, you may want to combine it with your language skills and find a special niche for yourself in the entertainment industry. As we have already mentioned, the number of radio programs, television shows, and movies broadcast in languages other than English is increasing all the time in the United States.

Music

The music business is a big part of the entertainment industry. If you want a career in the music industry, here are a few of your choices:

lyricist

musician

composer

vocalist

engineer

sound mixer

editor

producer

photographer

marketing-promotion specialist

tour manager

talent manager

talent agent

music publisher

technician

researcher

Movies

Hollywood has been exporting its fare for as long as movies have been made there. And many films from foreign shores invade the United States each year. Subtitles and overdubbing are the two main methods of translating languages used in films, from the badly dubbed Chinese kung fu movies of the 1970s to the more recent, literate subtitles of French new-wave films. Someone has to take the scripts and rework them to fit American lingo closely enough so that the audience is able to accept the method of translation with a degree of comfort.

Translation is the most obvious way to use your language skills in the movie industry, but it is by no means the only job for those with a second language. Actors need language skills for certain parts, and they need coaches to learn them. Non-native speakers may work with tutors to make their English sound more American. U.S. actors may need to develop a convincing foreign accent. And anyone employed in the industry may find chances to use their language skills off-screen while shooting on location in countries around the world.

A career in movies may mean work in any one of a dozen capacities. Here are a few of your options:

screenwriter

director

producer

photographer

cinematographer

on-screen talent

lighting technician

costumer

makeup artist

advertising salesperson

marketer

electrician

stunt performer

carpenter

driver

caterer

translator

voice coach

musician

composer

special effects expert

set designer

set decorator

Market Research

The mass media gets most of its revenue from advertising. Advertisers, in turn, want to know if their ads are pulling in customers. Sometimes a company wants to know if it is feasible to sell a given product in a specified market. To answer these questions, companies contract with firms that specialize in market research. Positions in market research almost always require advanced degrees. And fluency in another language is always a plus.

Consider the case of Hugh, who works for a market research firm. One west coast company wanted to introduce its product into South America. The product was aimed at adults between the ages of 24–36. The company arranged to have one-minute ads placed on three radio stations in Santiago, Chile. Hugh's firm was called in at that point to measure listener response. Hugh went to Santiago and discovered that there was no response at all. Not a single listener had requested the product!

Rather than return right away to the United States to give the bad news to the company that paid for the advertising, Hugh began to look into the reason for such a disastrous ad campaign. Through a friend of a friend, he talked it over with a Chilean who worked in a local ad agency. She lent Hugh a copy of a recent radio ratings study that listed the viewer audience for every radio station in the country. Here Hugh discovered that one of the three target radio stations catered to teenagers (not the target audience for the ad campaign) and another station to young adults, but not at the particular hour when the ads were broadcast. The third station was an appropriate one to reach the desired audience, but that station had not broadcast any of the commercials!

Hugh then cabled the U.S. company, outlining what had happened. He suggested different hours for the one station and other, substitute stations for future airing. These changes were made, the ads pulled, and Hugh was then able to develop profiles of those who responded compared to other listeners who did not respond to the ads.

This troubleshooting was only possible because Hugh speaks Spanish and knows his way around the block in Latin America. Many U.S. businesses sell to foreign markets and need market researchers abroad to help them understand the consumers they are trying to reach. Market research is another great way to find chances to travel abroad and use your language skills on the job.

Health Care Careers

*H*ealth care is one of the fastest growing and most human-resource-intensive industries in the United States and abroad. There are two broad job categories in health care: health diagnosing occupations and health assessment and treating occupations.

Health diagnosing occupations include these professionals:

chiropractors

dentists

optometrists

physicians

podiatrists

Health assessment and treating occupations include these professionals:

dietitians and nutritionists

occupational therapists

pharmacists

physical therapists

physician assistants

recreational therapists

registered nurses

respiratory therapists

speech-language pathologists and audiologists

All told, there are some 671,000 persons employed in health diagnosing positions and 2,063,000 persons employed in health assessment and treating occupations in this country. (The majority—1,577,000—of this latter category are registered nurses.) Knowledge of other languages is a distinct asset in all of these occupations.

Many health workers deal directly with people, and since increasing numbers of people needing health services in the United States speak something other than English as the primary language, the need for foreign language-capable people in the health professions is high.

There are many medical related tasks that require people who work behind the scenes using foreign language skills to help people get healthy and stay healthy. Following is a list of jobs and positions in health care:

dental assistant

dental hygienist

dietary aide

emergency medical technician

paramedic

hospital care investigator

practical nurse

registered nurse

physician

surgeon

Requirements

Before you investigate specific jobs, you should consider your attitude toward the health profession. Would you enjoy working with people who have health or emotional problems? Do you have the type of personality that would make you able to work in an atmosphere where conditions are often hectic and demand a combination of tact and decisiveness?

All of these professions require, of course, special training. The health-diagnosing occupations require doctorates. Four to six years of college—plus many hours of practicum—is generally the minimum level of training required for the health assessment and treating occupations.

There are, however, some health related occupations that require much less training. You may want to work in one of these jobs to get a better sense of health related work before you invest in the many years of training that many of the health occupations require. Some of these jobs are highlighted next.

Job Descriptions

If you are interested in a health care position, then the next step in your plan is to consider the opportunities that are available for you to use language skills that you have, or that you may develop, in health care jobs. Here is a description of some jobs in the health field that you can consider.

Ambulatory Care Technician

People in hospitals, clinics, and nursing homes who are unable to move around completely on their own power require technicians to help. When people can't walk and have trouble making their needs known because of language barriers, their frustration level rises. Your training in a foreign language, even if it is minimal, could help people both move around and communicate.

Biomedical Equipment Technician

More and more machines and instruments are being developed to test people and assist them with various kinds of ailments. People who operate these biomedical machines must be trained technicians. But they should also be "people" persons because people undergoing medical testing are often nervous and upset. If you can explain biomedical procedures quietly and effectively in the language with which the person is most comfortable, you will help the person, and you will help the whole team that is trying to make that person well.

Mental Health Assistant

The mental health assistant doesn't work with instruments and machines like the biomedical technician. But mental health assistants also need specialized training. They need skills in psychology and human behavior. With the increasing stress of modern society, with the high incidence of drug and alcohol related illnesses, there is a growing need for mental health assistants. If people have emotional problems, and also are unable to communicate to mental health workers because of language difficulties, their situation is obviously very serious. You can use mental health training and your language skills to help such people and perhaps move forward to a very rewarding career in the mental health profession.

Medical Record Clerk

You may be attracted to the health profession, but working directly with people may not be what you do best. That's fine because there are jobs in the health field where you can contribute much without dealing directly with the patients. With the vast number of immigrants, tourists, and foreign visitors to our country, we can expect that there will be health problems. All health problems need to be documented. You may find it rewarding to use your language skill in helping health care professionals translate health documents and health insurance forms into English.

Allied Health Professionals

This group of health care professionals includes respiratory, occupational, and physical therapists; radiology (x-ray) technicians; medical technologists; and phlebotomists (those who draw blood). All of these professions involve patient contact, and involve doing medical procedures that can be stressful and painful. Any second language skills will be invaluable in alleviating trauma to the patient. Speaking the patient's native language will enable the health care professional to do a better job, resulting in better medical care for the patient.

Patients who are able to communicate with their health care givers and to clearly understand what is being done to them, and why it is being done, are better able to cooperate with the procedure and less anxious about their treatment. As a health care worker, it is also extremely beneficial to be able to explain the procedure to the patient's family or friends. A second language skill that facilitates such communication can greatly ease the anxiety associated with health care.

Licensed Practical Nurse, Nurse's Aide

This group of health care workers has by far the greatest amount of patient contact. Nurses who have language skills that enable them to talk with their patients, and receive feedback from patients, are able to give the best possible care, with the best possible results.

Nurses also have the most interaction with the patient's family and friends, and clear communication with them can be crucial in establishing a medical history and in relieving anxiety and stress in both the patients and their loved ones. The nurse often serves as a go-between for the patient and the physician. Therefore, the clearer the clinical picture the nurse is able to obtain, the better the treatment the whole health care team can provide.

Emergency Medical Technician

These people respond to all sorts of emergencies. For reasons similar to those listed above, a second language ability that reflects the demographics of the area where they work can be a crucial, perhaps even life-saving, skill for EMTs. Since they must respond to emergency calls, EMTs are not always able to predict the language of the patient. Often the patient is unconscious, and in such cases communication with the family or witnesses of the accident can be vital to the success of treatment. This can be a very stressful occupation, but also a very rewarding one that offers an opportunity to use many skills, including second language capabilities.

Some organizations that need people with foreign language skills are CARE, Inc., the World Health Organization, Red Cross International, and the American Friends Service Committee.

For More Information

The following organizations should be helpful in gathering further information on health care careers. It is always a good idea to include a self-addressed stamped envelope with your request.

International Chiropractors Association
1110 North Glebe Road, Suite 1000
Arlington, VA 22201

Council on Chiropractic Education
4401 Westown Parkway, Suite 120
West Des Moines, IA 50265

American Dental Association
Council on Dental Education
211 East Chicago Avenue
Chicago, IL 60611

American Association of Dental Schools
1625 Massachusetts Avenue, N.W.
Washington, D.C. 20036

American Optometric Association
Educational Services
243 North Lindbergh Boulevard
St. Louis, MO 63141

Association of Schools and Colleges of Optometry
6110 Executive Boulevard, Suite 514
Rockville, MD 20852

American Medical Association
535 N. Dearborn Street
Chicago, IL 60610

Association of American Medical Colleges
Publications Department
One DuPont Circle, N.W.
Washington, D.C. 20036

American Osteopathic Association
Department of Public Relations
142 East Ontario Street
Chicago, IL 60611

American Association of Colleges of Osteopathic Medicine
6110 Executive Boulevard, Suite 405
Rockville, MD 20852

American Veterinary Medical Association
930 N. Meacham Road
Schaumburg, IL 60196

American Association of Veterinary Medicine Colleges
1023 15th Street, N.W., Third Floor
Washington, D.C. 20005

Health Assessment and Treating Occupations:

The American Dietetic Association
216 West Jackson Boulevard, Suite 800
Chicago, IL 60606

American Occupational Therapy Association
P.O. Box 1725
1383 Piccard Drive
Rockville, MD 20850

American Association of Colleges of Pharmacy
1426 Prince Street
Alexandria, VA 22314

American Society of Hospital Pharmacists
4630 Montgomery Avenue
Bethesda, MD 20814

American Physical Therapy Association
1111 North Fairfax Street
Alexandria, VA 22314

American Academy of Physician Assistants
950 North Washington Street
Alexandria, VA 22314

Association of Physician Assistant Programs
950 North Washington Street
Alexandria, VA 22314

National Therapeutic Recreation Society (a division of the
    National Recreation and Park Association)
3101 Park Center Drive
Alexandria, VA 22302

American Therapeutic Recreation Association
Associated Management Systems
P.O. Box 15215
Hattiesburg, MS 39403

Communications Department
National League for Nursing
350 Hudson Street
New York, NY 10014

National Student Nurses' Association
555 West 57 Street
New York, NY 10019
(Send $1 for a brochure entitled *Is Nursing for You?*)

American Nurses' Association
2420 Pershing Road
Kansas City, MO 64108

American Hospital Association
Division of Nursing
840 North Lake Shore Drive
Chicago, IL 60611

The National Board for Respiratory Care, Inc.
11015 West 75th Terrace
Shawnee Mission, KS 66214

American Speech-Language-Hearing Association
10801 Rockville Pike
Rockville, MD 20852

CHAPTER NINE

Travel and Tourism

The employment of travel agents, according to United States Department of Labor statistics, is expected to "grow much faster than the average for all occupations through the year 2000." Moreover, jobs related to travel, not just travel agents, are expected to grow as well. These include secretaries, tour guides, airline reservation agents, rental car agents, and travel agents and counselors.

About half of the country's 145,000 travel agents work in suburban areas, forty percent in large cities, and the remainder are spread throughout small towns and rural areas. Among their duties, travel agents serve clients who wish to travel internationally by providing information on customs regulations; required papers such as passports, visas, vaccination certificates; current exchange rates; and travel tips of all kinds.

Agents do get away from their desks occasionally to travel. Often they travel to foreign places as guests of a resort area. Resorts sponsor them so the agents can become more effective promoters of these areas. For example, one client asked Josh, a travel agent in a southern city, about hotels in the Bahamas. Josh suggested a Holiday Inn. The client balked, looking for something more upscale yet economical. Josh was able to describe the Nassau Holiday Inn accurately and appealingly because he himself had stayed there (as a guest of the hotel). The client took Josh's suggestion and returned from his vacation very pleased. Agents who can steer clients away from undesirable lodgings and toward better accommodations in the same price range are much prized by their clients.

The travel agent's work load varies, depending on the season and the economy. International business travel is fairly constant from month to month, but tourist travel is very heavy during vacation time, especially summer. Foreign travel to the United States is influenced by factors such as the strength of the dollar and special promotions. Naturally, more tourists visit the United States when the dollar is weak. Sometimes special events are widely publicized and may attract visitors.

One example of such a promotion centers on the historical significance of 1992, the 500th anniversary of the famous voyage of Columbus. The year 1992 will be remembered in the travel industry as the year the United States and the world celebrated this anniversary of Christopher Columbus arriving in the new world. Celebrations and commemorative ceremonies are scheduled all over this country. Spain has been selected to host the 1992 Olympics. Like the celebration of the American Bicentennial in 1976, the 1992 Quincentennial of the discovery of the New World offers a great opportunity to attract foreign visitors to the United States.

The Language Barrier

Tourism and foreign travel continue to grow in the United States. And one of the most common problems that foreign travelers experience is communication. International travel agents indicated in a survey that language is one of the most serious problems in attracting foreign travelers to the United States. The Illinois senator Paul Simon has noted, wryly, that the Immigration Service should erect a sign at our international airports:

Welcome to the United States.
We Do Not Speak Your Language.

An item on foreign visitors in the *New York Times* told of the difficulties people from abroad often encounter while visiting the United States. Many foreign visitors here suffer more than a little inconvenience, a great deal of it due to language problems. Most Americans cannot say even the most rudimentary guidebook phrases in any language save their own. Even more serious is the failure of so-called hospitality industries to provide adequate bilingual, not to mention multilingual, personnel. And the language difficulties serve to exacerbate ordinary day-to-day problems. One recent visitor complained to one of the authors that he, a Hindu, was unable to find good vegetarian meals in those parts of the United States where he traveled. No one had thought to provide a listing of restaurants where he could eat without violating his religious beliefs.

Progress has been made in the last twenty years. The United States has many more language-qualified people in the travel and tourism industry than there were in the 1970s. But there are still not enough to serve the vast numbers of foreign visitors who arrive each year. The travel and tourism industry needs language-qualified employees at all levels.

In terms of job prospects for people with the ability to speak more than one language, the potential is great. If you work for a travel agency, you can certainly help your U.S. clients more effectively if you are able to talk to people abroad in the language of their country, or at least in a language other than English.

Working Conditions

Travel agents spend most of their time working behind a desk—conferring with clients, punching alternate schedules into a computer in a search for the best rates and connections, making car rental and hotel reservations, and arranging for group travel. During peak travel times, agents typically are under a great deal of pressure, and, especially if they own their own business, they often work long hours. Pay for beginners is modest. Managers earn better salaries. The travel industry is sensitive to economic recessions when people tend to put off their travel plans.

Travel agents need good interpersonal skills. You need to be a good salesperson—pleasant, patient, and able to gain the confidence of your clients.

Training

Nobody is excited by the prospect of hiring an inexperienced travel agent, so how do you get trained? There are several options.

Many private vocational schools offer full-time programs lasting from three to twelve weeks. Some schools offer weekend and/or evening courses. There are even some colleges that offer a bachelor's or master's degree in travel and tourism.

Courses in foreign languages, geography, history, and computer use are useful for aspiring travel agents. If you want to start your own agency (you should be an experienced travel agent first), courses in accounting and business management also are helpful. Agencies like their employees to have a college degree (in anything), although this is often stated as a preference rather than a requirement.

In addition to courses offered by colleges and vocational schools, training is available from travel associations. The American Society of Travel Agents (ASTA) and the Institute of Certified Travel Agents offer a correspondence course. Once you become an experienced travel agent, you may want to take an advanced, eighteen-month, part-time course offered by the Institute of Certified Travel Agents. This gives you the title of Certified Travel Counselor. Another recognized mark of achievement is the certificate of proficiency offered by the American Society of Travel Agents to those who pass a three-hour examination.

Whatever course of study you choose, education is an important part of preparing to become a travel agent. Two other factors are also key to your success: work experience and travel. On-the-job training is invaluable. You may want to start by taking some courses and then applying for part-time work as an airline reservations clerk or receptionist in a travel agency. With experience and education, you will advance. If you can afford it, travel is another way to make yourself ready for a career as a travel agent. Firsthand experience of vacation spots allows you to better inform clients about what awaits them when they leave for their trip.

Related Job Opportunities

Airport Personnel

Working at an airport can give you an opportunity to practice your language and service skills. Everyone from bus drivers and "sky caps," to food service and security personnel may well be in frequent daily contact with people who don't speak English, and who need assistance or service. If you have people skills and some level of language capability, you can launch a career in tourism and travel by working an an airport.

Other opportunities to use foreign language skills come from working directly for the airlines. Pilots and flight attendants assigned to international routes have an obvious chance to speak a language other than English on the job. It takes time and training to be assigned to these positions of responsibility, but the work is well worth considering if you have language skills and an interest in flying. And although language skills are not required for these jobs, knowing another language does give job candidates an edge in a tough market. It also makes assignment to international flights more likely once you have secured a job with the airlines.

Hotels and Motels

Some large metropolitan hotels have employees who are fluent in as many as five different languages. These individuals serve as desk clerks, cashiers, in the front office, and in other positions. As travel tourism increases in the United States, the need for bilingual or multilingual personnel in the hospitality industry—hotels, motels, restaurants—has expanded from the elite metropolitan establishments to the small hotels, inns, and motels in towns and cities across America. The way foreign visitors are turning up in places like Lawrence, Kansas, and Pensacola, Florida, it is clear that English-only hotel and motel workers will be underprepared to serve future guests.

For More Information

For more details on travel careers, contact the following associations.

American Society of Travel Agents
1101 King Street
Alexandria, VA 22134

Airline Pilots Association, International
1625 Massachusetts Avenue, NW
Washington, DC 20036

Association of Flight Attendants
1625 Massachusetts Avenue, NW
Washington, DC 20036

The Institute of Certified Travel Agents
148 Lindon Street
P.O. Box 56
Wellesley, MA 02181

The Local and Federal Government

Virtually all the jobs described previously can be found in one form or another within the programs of the federal government: social sciences, librarianship, protection, translation, health care, and more. If you pursue any of these jobs within the federal system, most of what has already been discussed will still apply. In addition, there are unique requirements and responsibilities involved with working for the government.

The federal government represents the biggest bureaucracy in the world. You must be a team worker and be able to handle the red tape and intricacies of this huge enterprise. Some people enjoy the connections and interplay and learning to work with them instead of against them. If you are one of these people, government jobs can be very satisfying, and there are many varied opportunities for multilingual work.

Opportunities and Rewards

Working for the federal government is different from working anywhere else. If you are unsure about getting into government work, internships provide a good way to explore the option. Many branches of the federal government offer both paid and unpaid internships that will give you good firsthand knowledge of both multilingual and government work. Whether you choose to continue with a government career or decide it is not for you, the experience will prove very valuable in improving your language and job skills.

Employment opportunities within the federal government are greater and more far ranging and varied than most people realize. One of the most difficult parts of getting a job with the government is finding out about openings. One of the best ways to do this is to apply for job information from the specific department in which you wish to work.

The pay and advancement for all civil service jobs is very rigid and set by the very strict, structured guidelines of the GS system. Most language related jobs will fall in the GS-5 to GS-11 range which represents a pay scale of about $15,000–$30,000. There is a category of "excepted" jobs. Employees in excepted service jobs receive similar pay but are not subject to the same exam and testing procedures nor are they affected by other GS guidelines like extra points for veteran status. Excepted jobs are sometimes put up on limited contracts and sometimes last only for a finite contract period. Benefits such as retirement, saving plans, insurance, and leave are very good for civil service jobs and often these are extended to excepted service employees but not always.

With government jobs, there are requirements you won't often find if you apply for work elsewhere. Government jobs often require you to be finger-printed. When some level of security clearance is necessary, details of your past may be investigated, and you may be required to take a polygraph test. Many of the language related jobs will require travel, and that can be a disadvantage or an advantage depending on your point of view. Your working in the government may also restrict your involvement with various political parties to avoid conflicts of interest.

Language Proficiency

Language proficiency to qualify for a job is based heavily on tests. Most departments rely on the Foreign Service Institute or Inter Agency Language Round Table proficiency ratings which rate prospective employees from 0–5 according to the results of the testing. As we all know, written structured testing is not always the most accurate way of judging language and communication skills. And once hired, if your on the job performance does not match the level estimated by the testing procedure, they will let you go.

The U.S. Department of State has many jobs that require foreign language proficiency (usually at a 3.3 rating). The most common State Department programs that do are:

Foreign Service

Human Rights and Humanitarian Affairs

Bureau of Intelligence and Research

Refugee Programs

There are several other divisions attached to the State Department that also seek employees with foreign language skills. They are:

Agency for International Development

United States Information Agency

There are also language-related positions in other government agencies, including the Department of Defense, the National Security Agency, the Central Intelligence Agency, and the Immigration and Naturalization Service.

The particular languages most in demand depend on the political circumstances of the day. At this writing, the languages most in demand are Arabic (and dialects), Chinese (and dialects), Russian, Korean, Japanese, Farsi, and Polish.

In addition to Language skills, prospective government employees should have an interest in other cultures and in living abroad. They should be able to adapt quickly to the country where they are assigned. Sometimes this means adjustments in life-style. For example, Anthony, an employee of the Agency for International Development, was stationed in Afghanistan. He reports that one of the strains of living in Muslim countries is that it is considered gross by most local people to show any affection in public toward your wife. Hand holding and goodbye kisses are to be avoided like the plague. Even in the privacy of your home, you must exercise discretion because the servants may be offended and report the barbarian behavior to their friends and associates. Even so, Anthony was willing to adjust, and he enjoyed many fruitful years living in various Muslim countries.

For More Information

For more detailed information on jobs with the federal government, write to:

U.S. Department of State
Bureau of Personnel
Office of Recruitment, Examination, and Employment
Washington, D.C. 20520

Law Enforcement, Corrections, and Fire Fighting

Police officers and related personnel, corrections officers and fire fighters render vital services to any community, and persons in these occupations are generally highly respected. There are, of course, dangers associated with these jobs, and they should be given serious consideration when you are contemplating a job in protective services or corrections.

These jobs can be dangerous and stressful for both those working in the field and for their families. You need to consider that your work will bring you into contact with many of the most unpleasant aspects of our society, and it takes a toughness to face the work day after day. At the same time, your direct service to people of your community offers many satisfactions. Your contributions to your community and to society are concrete, and many find great satisfaction in these jobs.

Requirements and Training

For all of the jobs described above, it is necessary to have a high school diploma or the equivalent. You must also be a U.S. citizen. Training beyond high school is also required, and the length and type of training will depend on the job you are seeking. Many universities and community colleges offer one- and two-year programs in law enforcement and related fields, and police, fire, and correction departments offer training academies. The need for bilingual and multilingual skills in these occupations is very apparent, especially in large metropolitan areas. Workers need to first have good written and verbal communication skills in English. Gathering data, interviewing witnesses, record keeping, taking notes, and writing clear concise reports are important parts of all these occupations.

Many of the people encountered daily in large cities will not speak English as their primary language, and some will not speak it at all. For law enforcement personnel, being able to communicate with these people in their primary language has many advantages. And possessing the language skills necessary to do so will make you very valuable and improve your performance and safety on the job. Your language skills need to be such that people speaking with you will be confident that they are being understood, and you must be sure you are understood by them as well. Here school book perfection is not required; it's knowing the language of the street and the expressions of the specific subcultures with which you will be dealing that is important. Employers are especially seeking people from the minority groups that they will serve. In times of stress and danger, language can be the difference between life and death, and the benefits are enhanced when the officer or firefighter not only speaks the language but is identifiable as a member of the community ethnic group. Current literature and projections for the future specifically mention a great need for Hispanic and Chinese language proficiencies and backgrounds in these professions.

Police Enforcement

Police officers are increasingly required to exhibit social and cultural sensitivity. If you have an interest in law enforcement at the local, state, or national level, your efforts will be enhanced by language and cultural skills. Even in small communities in rural settings, police and sheriff's department personnel are being hired because of their skill in a second language. At the state level, the highway patrol and state investigative agencies are seeking officers and detectives with language skills. The FBI and other federal government law enforcement organizations all have policies that call for increased numbers of second language qualified personnel.

Recently, a riot erupted in Washington, D.C. when an English-speaking policewoman arrested an inebriated Spanish-speaking man one weekend in a park in the Hispanic area of the city. The arrested man and his friends didn't see anything wrong with getting drunk in the park on a Sunday afternoon. Several million dollars of property damage resulted, and a curfew was in effect for a week. Tensions had built up in the Hispanic community over what they regarded as heavy-handed police tactics. Significantly, of the five thousand or so police officers in the District, fewer than a hundred spoke Spanish at the time, and few of these were stationed in the Spanish-speaking parts of the city. Hiring officers with second-language skills can be a very cost effective move and a good way to help improve the relationship between the police and the community in tense times.

Corrections

People who work in the protective services and correctional centers should have a strong sense of social justice and responsibility. Corrections officers work with people who have broken the law or have had some other brush with the legal system. Here the need is for people who can explain laws and legal terms to persons whose primary language is not English. As the crime rate continues to increase, more people are needed in law enforcement and corrections positions.

Fire Fighters

Like law enforcement personnel, fire fighters are found in all communities and are responsible to protect all segments of the community. In big cities where there are large foreign language communities concentrated in certain areas, it may be a matter of life or death for fire fighters to be able to understand victims of fires or explosions who are trying to tell them about friends and loved ones who are trapped or in danger.

There was a recent fire in an apartment building in Washington, D.C. Most of the building's inhabitants were Spanish-speaking people from Central America. None of the fire fighters on the scene spoke Spanish, so their instructions to the building's inhabitants were not understood. In this job, a lack of communication can be life-threatening.

CHAPTER ELEVEN

Language-Intensive Jobs: Translating, Interpreting, Teaching

Translating, interpreting, and teaching are jobs people tend to think of first when seeking ways to use their foreign language skills. These occupations all require exceptional written and oral fluency in the target language.

Translating and Interpreting

Translators and interpreters transfer information from one language into another. Translators work with written information, and interpreters with spoken information. Both try to achieve a minimum of distortion in the process. Not only should the message of the translation or interpretation be the same as the original, but the style and emotional content of the statement should be comparable to the original. A good translator or interpreter does not impose his or her own style, interpretation, or opinion onto the translation or interpretation.

There are about 10,000 translators and interpreters working in the United States, many working only part time. The market tendency seems to favor interpreters over translators. In the

State Department, for example, contract interpreters number around 1,200, while contract translators number around 200. Both translators and interpreters require the highest level of second language skills. Translators almost always translate from the second language into their native language, but this is not always the case with interpreters. Both of these occupations require extensive knowledge of the native language as well as the second language. Translators must be meticulous students of language patterns, grammar, and idiomatic meaning. Persons interested in interpretation should be good with people, good listeners, and have clear speech. Both translators and interpreters will be in greater demand and have more interesting jobs if they are interested in a wide range of subjects, and are knowledgeable in a variety of areas. Some interpreters work in the court systems, usually on a free-lance basis, translating the depositions of non-English–speaking witnesses, and providing translations for the defendants.

Neyde supplements her income as a college teacher by on-call interpreting for the local courts during her vacations. She finds this free-lance interpreting (in Portuguese, Spanish, French, and Italian), challenging and really interesting. One thing to note is that the hourly pay differs according to the language. For example, Neyde is paid over twice the amount for Portuguese as for Spanish. To get these jobs, she registered with different agencies, such as the Immigration and Naturalization Service.

An important skill for translators is to know the various resources available to find information. Research is an important part of this job. If you are interested in lots of things, have excellent primary and secondary language skills, and like meeting new people or writing, this might be the career for you.

Employers

The federal government is the largest single employer of translators and interpreters. These federal agencies include the State Department, the FBI, National Security Agency, Central Intelligence Agency, Agency for International Development, Library of Congress, and the U.S. Information Agency. Other employers include the United Nations, international agencies such as the International Development Bank, the Telecommunications Satellite Organization, the Organization of American States, the Pan-American Health Organization, and some private industries. Frequently, translators will be self-employed, people who are contracted by companies to translate a personnel manual or a piece of business correspondence. Large international companies such as IBM have full-time translators on board. Guadalupe, an English-Spanish-Portuguese translator working for an international electronic firm, specializes in technical documents and has a team of translators working under her. Translators and interpreters will have more job opportunities if they know several languages.

Most American service organizations and businesses do not employ translators, but their translations are provided by employees whose primary job is not language related. These employers consider a second language a very valuable secondary skill.

Free-lance translators are generally paid by the number of words (or pages), either in the original or the translation. Rates vary from $20 to $100 per thousand words. A good free-lance translator can earn a decent living and enjoy the benefit of a flexible work schedule.

Job Requirements

The same high-level language skills required by translation are also needed to work as an interpreter, with the added necessity of a fluency with the spoken work. Nuance and accent can be very important in oral communication. Employers of interpreters are usually high government or business officials. Therefore an understanding of protocol, customs, and etiquette is essential for interpreters who wish to efficiently and unobtrusively facilitate conversation between the parties they are interpreting for.

Persons interested in careers in this area need more than a knowledge of a second language. Translators and interpreters alike should read widely in the language they will be translating. Newspapers, magazines, catalogs, and general materials of all sorts are helpful. Travel in countries where the language is spoken is invaluable, especially for the interpreter. Most interpreters have spoken several languages all of their lives. United Nations interpreters need native or near-native fluency in at least three of the six official languages of the UN: Arabic, Chinese, English, French, Russian, and Spanish. These positions are very competitive.

The translator will need courses in journalism and technical writing. Familiarity with the jargon of many fields will greatly enhance the value of a translator or interpreter. There are special translator/interpreter training programs at some universities. Russian, German, Japanese, French, and Spanish are the languages most in demand. There is a growing need for interpreters and translators in Portuguese, Chinese, and Arabic. A couple of broad areas of knowledge (math, science, business) as well as extensive language skills will enable the interpreter or translator to have the greatest number of career options.

Foreign Language Teaching

We are all familiar with foreign language teaching; most of us have enrolled in foreign language classes. Many of you may have been inspired to use your second language by one of the 50,000 grade school, high school, or college foreign language teachers. In the current job market, these teaching jobs are quite competitive. On the college level, they require a bachelor's degree, and often a master's degree, plus teacher certification which often involves one or two years of education courses. Many private schools do not require teacher certification.

About 20 percent of elementary schools and 90 percent of secondary schools offer foreign language instruction. Most of these jobs are for Spanish, French, German, and Latin, in descending order of popularity. Career opportunities on the college level are scarce, since most students are taught by graduate assistants, especially at the larger universities.

Bilingual Education Programs

Currently, it is easier to find jobs in bilingual education than it is in foreign language teaching. Bilingual programs are for students from non-English–speaking homes who will profit from having subject matter taught in a language they can understand. Bilingual teachers, most of whom are employed on the primary school level, may teach science, math, social studies, or language arts—in the students' native language.

Employers (school superintendents and principals) look for people who are fluent in the requisite language. This is usually Spanish, but on occasion may be any one of a hundred other languages. Prospective bilingual teachers need to have a college degree (or two) and be interested in taking the education courses needed to gain state certification if they do not already posses it. If you are interested in teaching in a bilingual program, and there is a Hispanic or other ethnic community in your area whose language and culture you know, call the local school superintendent to find out the prospects. A related field, teaching English as a second language, was the subject of chapter 3 in this book.

Anthropology

There are other teachers who often find fluency in a second language to be especially useful. Anthropologists and political scientists are two examples.

Anthropologists study the origins, cultures, traditions, beliefs, politics, and social relationships of the world's people. They often live abroad for extended periods, often in "primitive" societies, and they may hold teaching positions in universities or colleges. A Ph.D. is generally required.

Political Science

Political scientists study government at all levels, from the smallest native village to the international community of nations. Foreign language skills are important not only to those who are concerned with international relations and foreign political systems, but also to those interested in the dynamics of local politics.

Crosscultural and ethnic/linguistic interaction plays an important part in local elections, community development plans, and community solidarity efforts. If you have special interest in politics, the development of your language and cultural skills can help move your career plans forward.

For More Information

American Association of Language Specialists
1000 Connecticut Avenue, N.W., Suite 9
Washington, D.C. 20036

American Literary Translators Association
Box 830688, MC35
University of Texas
Dallas, TX 75083

American Society of Interpreters
P.O. Box 9603
Washington, D.C. 20016

American Translators Association
109 Croton Avenue
Ossining, NY 10562

Society of Federal Linguists
P.O. Box 7765
Washington, D.C. 20044

American Council on the Teaching of Foreign Languages
   (ACTFL)
6 Executive Plaza
Yonkers, NY 10701

Office of Civilian Personnel
Defense Language Institute
Presidio of Monterey, CA 93944

National Clearinghouse for Bilingual Education
1118 22nd Street, N.W.
Washington, D.C. 20037

National Association for Bilingual Education (NABE)
Union Center Plaza
810 First Street, N.E., Third Floor
Washington, D.C. 20002

CHAPTER TWELVE

Consulting

*I*f you have some particular expertise which is in demand internationally, you may want to explore employment as an international consultant. You should possess a graduate degree related to your specialization and speak the language of the country that needs your expertise.

What expertise is in demand? Rural health care (including nutrition, family planning), rural educational development (mostly primary school level, including adult literacy), agriculture (including irrigation techniques), community development, civil engineering, and management (including computer science and accounting) are all areas where experienced consultants are needed.

Government priorities, along with skirt lengths, change. For example, specialists in small entrepreneurial business or in private nonprofit groups became an Agency for International Development priority in the late 1980s. No one can predict for certain which specializations will be in demand in the coming decades.

Requirements

How experienced do you have to be? Usually about ten years of experience is needed to be competitive as a consultant. Frequently, previous work in the host country is highly desirable.

What's this about advanced degrees? To be competitive for most of these opportunities, you must not only be able to do the job, you must be able to convince a stranger reading your curriculum vitae (a long, more academic type of resume) that your education and training equip you to do the job. In other words, you have to inspire confidence on paper. A master's degree is generally the lowest level of academic preparation sought; a Ph.D. is better.

What languages are generally required? For much of Africa, English and French (depending on which language the colonial power spoke) are all that most agencies can realistically require. Fluency in particular African languages (there are hundreds) would be an asset for community development work where that language is spoken, but this is rarely required.

One of the authors was attending an international conference in Kinshasa, Zaire. The author—along with two African colleagues, each from a different country—needed to make some logistical arrangements with two young men who were assigned this type of duty. The one colleague began, "Bwana, . . . ," in Swahili, a common East African *lingua franca.* The two men did not understand. The colleague then began in another language. They didn't understand this either. He then tried two other African languages. Same result. Then the other colleague tried five languages that he spoke. Same result. The author threw in another four European languages. Same result. At that point, the Swahili-speaking colleague made an unmistakable gesture meaning, "Well, what can you speak, dummy?" The two men drew themselves up with some pride, and each counted off on his fingers five or six languages. There were over 25 different languages spoken by the five men, and not one language in common!

Spanish is a requirement for much of Latin America, Portuguese for Brazil. Occasionally, an Indian language is useful. Consultants fluent in an Asian language have a distinct advantage in landing assignments in their culture area.

Opportunities and Rewards

Who hires international consultants? The companies that got most of the business a few years ago (as reported by Krannich and Krannich, 1990) are listed in appendix B.

From this list, you can earmark some companies that may be in need of someone with your special skills from time to time. To determine what other companies on the list do, consult the business section or reference section of your local library. Some of these companies may not now be doing as much international business as they were a few years ago, and others may have changed their focus somewhat. Similarly, there may be new players in international consulting. You can bring yourself up to date on your trip to the library.

Many of these companies keep a bank of resumes on hand (unlike most companies), and they will welcome receiving yours. You will, however, have to follow up all your leads. Arrange for an interview, and then follow up again periodically. A basic question concerns your availability: a few weeks, or months, at a time; or summers only?

A typical short-term assignment overseas as a consultant may involve working intensively with several people from the funding agency and a larger number of host nationals on a four- to six-week project. The contracts often stipulate a long list of tasks that must be completed. The hours are long; the real (if unpaid) workweek often is seven days. Your task may be to figure out how to get the project's objectives accomplished within the Ministry of Agriculture of Zimbabwe, without rubbing people the wrong way. Sometimes a fifty- to hundred-page report must be written and approved by the funding source.

Some agencies (AID, for example) calculate your daily wage by taking your annual income divided by 260 work days in a year. If you can document annual income from your job and/or other consulting contracts of, say, $30,000, your authorized daily rate would be $115. There are rarely any fringe benefits other than a per diem which differs according to living costs in the host country. Typically a per diem would run around $100 per day, much of which might be eaten up by hotel costs.

How do you get a consulting contract? The majority of the consulting contracts are let to large companies. They get their consultants by looking through their bank of curriculum vitaes and by calling contacts who suggest names to them. You must sell yourself to the company who will then submit your curriculum vitae to the funding agency (usually with two or three other CVs of qualified people). Then the funding agency selects from among the two to four CVs the consultant they want.

Some longer-term contracts also are let for periods of between one and five years. The salaries are generally good, and there are generous housing allowances.

Starting Your Own Consulting Business

Unless you are well known and/or well connected, starting your own business is a hard route to go. Most agencies, in spite of professed interest in small companies, want to contract with large companies or universities. Mark free-lanced for many years, receiving many contracts from several government agencies as a short-term consultant abroad. However, when he started his own international consulting firm, the agencies would not give his company any contracts. Mark complained to the small business advocacy departments within these agencies and was told that "Yes, we encourage small companies to solicit projects. But your company is a start-up company." Another company which has revenues of about two million a year was told by another government agency to go in with another, bigger company, because the agency didn't want to deal with such a small business. Your best bet is to get your contracts through an established company.

For more information on careers in international consulting, see the bibliography at the end of the next chapter.

CHAPTER THIRTEEN

Refining Your Job Search Strategy

M ichael J. Marquardt, the head of World Center for Development and Training (Arlington, Virginia) and a specialist in strategies for finding international jobs, identifies six steps in locating a job:

1. Develop a resume

2. Identify the job market

3. Identify contacts

4. Telephone for an informational interview—not a job

5. Interview for information

6. Interview for the job

These are indeed the basics of most good job search strategies; and we will review them in this chapter.

Develop a Resume

The purpose of a resume is not to get the job, it is to get an *interview* which may lead to a job. And when you go to the interview, you want to take another copy of your resume with you. Going to an interview without a resume in your pocket is a big mistake.

What is the best way to create a resume? First, it is crucial to know your own qualifications. Do you have the background and skills that are valued by the people who will hire you in your international job? If so, you will want to highlight these skills in your resume.

Next, it's important to have a career objective. Many resumes state a career objective at the beginning. Often the best place for a specific objective is in a cover letter rather than in the resume. (You don't want to limit your options, do you?) Still, it is a good idea to include a general career objective on your resume that is specific enough to show that you have a definite goal. Then you can state a more specific objective in each cover letter.

There are two general formats for resumes: chronological and functional. A chronological sequence is probably best for most young college graduates, or if you have followed a steady career progression in the same or related fields. If you have been out of the work force for some time, if your career has had long interruptions, or if you are making a drastic change in careers, then the functional format may be best for you. In this format you focus on achievements and skills. If you are in doubt of which format to use, use the chronological format. It is more conservative, and the people who do the hiring tend to be conservative themselves.

Once you have reviewed your qualifications, formulated an objective, and selected a resume format, it's time to focus on language. Clear, concise, and active are the key concepts here. You want to sound professional, intelligent, and warm. It is so easy to fall into boring prose and irritating jargon that it will be worth your while to pick up a manual or two on writing resumes. (See the bibliography at the end of this chapter.) There are a number of helpful software programs to enable you to turn out a professional-looking resume on a personal computer. Whatever you do, don't misspell any words, and don't lie about your work or educational background.

While you must be honest, you do want to play up your strengths. Describe what skills and accomplishments you had in your jobs (if they are relevant to the kind of job you are trying to get). American executives love "hard numbers." Quantify anything that you can: You were one of two secretaries in a department of eight professional epidemiologists, handling an average of 86 pieces of correspondence and 120 requests for information weekly over a computer network linking 843 health centers specializing in 14 contagious diseases. You get the point. And it is equally important to disguise your weaknesses. Some things that are generally considered weaknesses include staying less than three years in a job and being between jobs for more than a few months at a time. These can be finessed by omitting some jobs you were in for only a short time and by rounding off dates to just the year.

If you studied or travelled between jobs, be sure to make that clear. If you did volunteer work, by all means list it. Unpaid experience should be described in the same ways that you describe paid job experience. And don't forget to quantify.

You will want to include a section on education in your resume. If you are straight out of school or if you have a doctorate, list the education section first. If not, list it after the section on professional experience. If you have a college degree, omit reference to your high school experience (unless you were the valedictorian). List your college grade point average only if it was quite high. Don't list extra-curricular activities unless they have a direct bearing on the job you are trying to get. If you attended college for less than one year, then list the relevant courses.

Be very selective about the "optional" information you include on your resume. By all means include any special skills (computer skills, foreign languages) or professional awards. But think twice before you list anything that will turn off a conservative employer. Avoid controversy if you can. If your volunteer experience is with political or social groups that may be seen as controversial, you might want to generalize. You could mention that you were involved in civic affairs and community-development projects without naming names. Better still, exclude these items unless they are directly relevant to the job you are seeking.

Finally, you will want to make your resume easy to read. Keep it brief—one or two pages if you possibly can. Prospective employers tend to read only one page. Use white or beige paper (use 20- or 24-pound paper) and blank ink. Provide white space (margins). And use a standard type style (not script or Olde English).

Cover Letters

Always send a one-page, single spaced, cover letter with your resume. The letter should state your case, explaining what job you want and why.

Make the letter look great. It should be neat—with no spelling or grammar errors—and concise. Use plain paper; no letterheads unless you own the company.

Address the letter to a specific person, not to a job title. If you don't know the person's name and title, call the company's switchboard and ask the receptionist.

Like the resume, the cover letter should be brief, usually three paragraphs. In the first, catch the reader's attention: "Your advertisement in The Wall Street Journal caught my eye." Mention your objective in the first paragraph. In the second paragraph, sell your accomplishments. Quantify where you can. In the final paragraph, be specific about your plans to contact the organization after they receive your letter. Don't wait to hear from them! Initiative is appreciated and conveys enthusiasm.

Identify the Job Market

What kind of a job are you looking for? There are five kinds of international organizations:

1. Public multinational (The United Nations, The World Bank, The International Monetary Fund, The Organization of American States, The European Common Market, The North Atlantic Treaty Organization, The Organization for Economic Cooperation and Development)

2. Government (Department of State, Department of Defense, U.S. military forces, U.S. Information Agency, Agency for International Development, Department of Agriculture, Central Intelligence Agency, National Security Agency, Peace Corps)

3. Business (banks, manufacturing companies, consulting firms)

4. Educational (American Field Service, Council on International Educational Exchange, Institute on International Education, foundations, universities).

5. Private voluntary (CARE, Save the Children, Foster Parents Plan, The Salvation Army, The YMCA International Division)

It's important to understand the kind of employee each type of organization seeks. For example, unless you have years of relevant experience and prestigious university degrees, public multinationals are difficult to break into. Some government agencies are extremely competitive also. For example, only one in 93 applicants to the State Department gets a job there. The Peace Corps, contrary to the popular image, accepts people of all ages—if they have skills that are needed in developing nations. Two adventurous friends of the authors, Ralph and Jean, married for 50 years, got Peace Corps assignments together in Tonga. Businesses generally want you to spend a year or so in the United States, learning what the company is all about, before sending you trekking to an overseas post. Educational and private voluntary organizations often require special contacts to smooth the way to an international job.

Ask friends, and friends of friends, for ideas. What companies might hire for overseas work? Ask the local reference librarian for leads. Then start to zero in on them.

Identify Contacts

Once you evaluate in what general field you want to get a job, ask yourself several questions. Where do people in this field get together? How am I going to meet them? Who are the wheeler-dealers in the field? The answers are simple.

The logical place where practitioners in a field get together is at their annual conferences or trade shows. How do you find out where these are? Go to the library, and read the trade journals. Often there are a number of conferences: pick one that's close to you. So you go to the annual conference, now how do you meet the right people? This is where skimming those trade journals comes in handy. You jot down the names of some of the people who have published articles you enjoyed. You look for them on the program. Then you talk to them afterwards. ("I really enjoyed your article on community development projects in Papua New Guinea. . . .") You ask them to suggest leads for you to follow. (" Where should I begin to look for a job that will lead to an overseas posting in community development?")

Informational Interviews

Next you will want to talk to someone and continue your networking. Once you have identified several contacts (sometimes it takes just one, but the more the better), the next step is to call someone who is strategically placed in the field.

In effect, you call someone whom your contact has identified and say something like this: "Ms. Wilson, Dr. Brown suggested I contact you. He said you could be helpful in me to the field. Can you see me for 10 or 15 minutes?"

Most people will grant a brief interview under these circumstances. Occasionally, they will suggest you talk to someone else. Fine. Tell that other person the Dr. Brown suggested you call.

The Interview

There are three phases to any interview: preparation, the interview, and follow-up.

PREPARATION. Learn something about the person you are going to interview, and something about his or her organization. Jot down a few questions to ask ("What job do you think someone of my background might qualify for?" "What's the current job market in this area?" "Can you suggest some people I could talk to about the field?")

INTERVIEW. Listen carefully, be polite and at ease. Focus on the interview. Don't look out the window or appear bored or distracted. Be ready to leave without delay when you get a signal that the contact person wants to get back to his or her work.

FOLLOW-UP. Do send a thank you note. Your contact person didn't have to take time out of his or her schedule to see you. If you get a job as a result of another contact the person gave you, note it and thank the person for that, too.

Lois wanted a job in the Washington, D.C., area that would involve working with Asian refugees. She didn't know what kind of job her background would qualify her for, much less where to apply for a job. One of her professors gave Lois the name of a Mr. Chin, a prominent person in the field of intercultural communication who worked in the Washington area. Lois called, used her professor's name, and asked for an interview. The professor was known to Mr. Chin and Chin readily agreed to a meeting. During the meeting, Mr. Chin went out of his way to suggest several general categories of jobs for which Lois would be qualified. Then he suggested several agencies she might want to contact. Lois went to the one that looked most interesting, told the director that Mr. Chin had suggested she contact them, and a week later Lois was working for the agency.

Job Interviews

Many books have been written about successful techniques for job interviews. (They are similar to those used in informational interviews.) Some good sources are listed below. Read one or two of them, then go for it! There are many international jobs out there for foreign language aficionados.

For More Information

These books will give you more detailed information on job searches.

Bloch, Deborah Perlmutter. *How to Have a Winning Job Interview*. Lincolnwood, Ill: VGM Career Horizons, 1992.
Bolles, Richard N. *What Color Is Your Parachute? A Practical Manual for Job-Hunters & Career-Changers*. Berkeley: Ten Speed Press, 1990 ed.

Impact Publications
International Careers Department
4580 Sunshine Court
Woodbridge, VA 22192
(Request their free catalog.)

Karannich, Ronald L. and C. R. Krannich. *The Complete Guide to International Jobs and Careers*. Woodbridge, VA: Impact Publications, 1990.
Schuman, Howard. *Making It Abroad: The International Job Hunting Guide*. New York: Wiley, 1988.
Schuman, Nancy and William Lewis. *Revising Your Résumé*. New York: Wiley, 1986.

A P P E N D I X   A

State Offices of Volunteerism

Alabama
Governor's Office of Volunteerism
560 S. McDonough
Montgomery, AL 36130

Arkansas
Arkansas Office of Volunteerism
P.O. Box 1437
Little Rock, AR 72203-1437

Canada
(Not an S.O.V.)
Department of the Secretary of State of Canada
Ottawa, Ontario, Canada K1A 0M5

Connecticut
Governor's Council on Voluntary Action
80 Washington Street
Hartford, CT 06106

Delaware
Division of Volunteer Services
Department of Community Affairs
P.O. Box 1401
Dover, DE 19903

Florida
Volunteer Services
Dept. of Health and Rehabilitation Services
1321 Windwood Boulevard
Building 1, Room 216
Tallahassee, FL 32301

Georgia
Georgia Office of Volunteer Services
Department of Community Affairs
1200 Equitable Building
100 Peachtree Street, N.W.
Atlanta, GA 30303

Hawaii
Statewide Volunteer Services
Office of the Governor
State Capitol, Room 442
Honolulu, HI 96813

Illinois
Governor's Office of Voluntary Action
100 W. Randolph, 16th Floor
Chicago, IL 60601

Indiana
Governor's Voluntary Action Program
1 North Capitol
Indianapolis, IN 46204

Iowa
Governor's Office for Volunteers
State Capitol
Des Moines, IA 50319

Kentucky
Kentucky Office of Volunteer Services
275 East Main, 6W
Frankfort, KY 40601

Maine
Maine State Office of Volunteerism
State House Station 73
Augusta, ME 04333

Maryland
Governor's Office on Volunteerism
301 West Preston Street
Room 1501
Baltimore, MD 21201

Massachusetts
No S.O.V.

Minnesota
Minnesota Office on Volunteer Services
Department of Administration
500 Rice Street
St. Paul, MN 55155

Mississippi
No S.O.V.

Missouri
Missouri Volunteers
c/o Western Missouri Mental Health Center
600 East 22nd St.
Kansas City, MO 64108

Missouri Volunteers
c/o D.F.S.
615 East 13th St.
Kansas City, MO 64106

Nebraska
No S.O.V.

Nevada
No S.O.V.

New Hampshire
Governor's Office on Volunteerism
The State House
Concord, NH 03301

New Jersey
New Jersey Office of Volunteerism
The State House
CN001
Trenton, NJ 08625

New Mexico
Director of Constituent Services
State Capitol
Santa Fe, NM 87503

New York
Governor's Office for Voluntary Service
2 World Trade Center—57 Floor
New York, NY 10047

North Carolina
Governor's Office of Citizen Affairs
116 W. Jones Street
Raleigh, NC 27611

North Dakota
Office of Volunteer Services
Dept. of Human Services
Judicial Wing—3rd Floor
600 East Boulevard Avenue
Bismarck, ND 58505

Ohio
Ohio Office of Volunteerism
65 East State St., Room 1612
Columbus, OH 43266-0401

Oregon
Assistant to the Governor for Special Projects
State Capitol Building—Room 160
Salem, OR 97310

State Coordinator
Dept. of Human Resources Volunteer Program
1158 Chemeketa
Salem, OR 97310

Pennsylvania
Penn-SERVE
Governor's Office of Citizen's Service
Room 1304
Labor & Industry Building
Harrisburg, PA 17120

Rhode Island
Volunteer in Action, Inc.
160 Broad Street
Providence, RI 02903-4028

South Carolina
Volunteer Services Liaison
Office of the Governor
1205 Pendleton Street
Columbia, SC 29201

South Dakota
South Dakota Office of Volunteerism
State Capitol Building
Pierre, SD 57501

Tennessee
Administrative Services
Tennessee Dept. of Human Services
400 Deadrich Street
Nashville, TN 37248

Texas
Governor's Office of Community Leadership/Volunteer
   Services
P.O. Box 12428
Austin, TX 78711

Vermont
Director of Public Information
Governor's Action Line
109 State St.
Montpelier, VT 05602

Virginia
Virginia Department of Volunteerism
223 Governor St.
Richmond, VA 23219

Washington
Washington State Center for Voluntary Action
9th and Columbia Bldg., MS/GH-51
Olympia, WA 98504

West Virginia
No S.O.V.

Wyoming
(Not on S.O.V.)

Wyoming Volunteer Assistance Corp.
Box 4008, University Station
Laramie, WY 82071

APPENDIX B

Employers of International Consultants

Academy for Educational Development
1255 23rd Street, NW
Washington, DC 20037

Advanced Technology Inc.
12005 Sunrise Valley Drive
Reston, VA 22091

Adventist Development and Relief Agency
12501 Old Columbia Pike
Silver Spring, MD 20904

African American Labor Center
1400 K Street, NW, Suite 700
Washington, DC 20005

Aricare
440 R Street, NW
Washington, DC 20001

Agricultural Cooperative Development International
50 F Street, NW, Suite 900
Washington, DC 20001

American Institute for Free Labor Development
1015 20th Street, NW, 5th Floor
Washington, DC 20036

The Asia Foundation
465 California Street
San Francisco, CA 94104

Associates in Rural Development Inc.
PO Box 1397
Burlington, VT 05402

Association for Voluntary Surgical Contraception
122 E. 42nd Street
New York, NY 10168

Berger, Louis, International, Inc.
100 Halsted Street
East Orange, NJ 07019

Black and Veatch, Engineers-Architects
8400 Ward Parkway
PO Box 8405
Kansas City, MO 64114

Catholic Relief Services
209 W. Fayette Street
Baltimore, MD 21201

Cheacchi and Company Consulting
1730 Rhode Island Avenue, NW, Suite 910
Washington, DC 20036

Cooperative for American Relief Everywhere (CARE)
660 First Avenue
New York, NY 10016

Cooperative Housing Foundation
PO Box 91280
Washington, DC 20090

Education Development Center
55 Chapel Street
Newton, MA 02160

Family Health International
PO Box 13950
Durham, NC 27709

Institute for Development Anthropology
99 Collier Street
PO Box 2207
Binghamton, NY 13902-2207

International Executive Service Corps
Eight Stamford Forum
PO Box 10005
Stamford, CT 06904-2005

International Fertilizer Development Center
PO Box 2040
Muscle Shoals, AL 35660

International Food Policy Research Institute
1776 Massachusetts Avenue
Washington, DC 20036

Helen Keller International
15 W. 16th Street
New York, NY 10011

Little, Arthur D., Inc.
25 Acorn Park
Cambridge, MA 02140

Nathan Associates, Inc.
1301 Pennsylvania Avenue
Washington, DC 20004

National Academy of Sciences
2101 Constitution Avenue, NW
Washington, DC 20418

National Research Council
2101 Constitution Avenue, NW
Washington, DC 20418

Parsons Brinckerhoff Quad and Douglas Inc.
One Penn Plaza
New York, NY 10119

Pathfinder Fund
Nine Galen Street, Suite 217
Watertown, MA 02172

People-to-People Health Foundation
Project HOPE Health Sciences
Education Center
Millwood, VA 22646

Planning and Development Collaborative International
    (PADCO)
1012 N Street, NW
Washington, DC 20001

Population Council
One Dag Hammarskjold Plaza
New York, NY 10017

Population Reference Bureau
777 14th Street, NW, Suite 800
Washington, DC 20005

Pragma International
1050 17th Street, NW
Washington, DC 20036

Price Waterhouse
1251 Avenue of the Americas
New York, NY 10020

Research Triangle Institute
PO Box 12194
Research Triangle Park, NC 27709-2194

Save the Children Federation
54 Wilton Road
Westport, CT 06880

Tropical Research and Development
519 NW 60th Street, Suite D
Gainesville, FL 32607

United Nations Childrens Fund (UNICEF)
Three United Nations Plaza
New York, NY 10017

Urban Institute
2100 M Street, NW
Washington, DC 20037

World Wildlife Fund
1250 24th Street, NW
Washington, DC 20037